Do Unto Others

Do Unto Others

*How Good Deeds Can
Change Your Life*

RABBI ABRAHAM J. TWERSKI, M.D.

**Andrews McMeel
Publishing**

Kansas City

Library of Congress Cataloging-in-Publication Data

98 99 00 01   EBA   10 9 8 7 6 5 4 3 2

Twerski, Abraham J.
    Do onto others : how good deeds can change your life / Abraham J. Twerski.
        p. cm.
    ISBN 0-8362-3597-5 (hardcover)
    I. Altruism. I. Title
BJ1474.T84   1997
170'.44—dc21   97-18854
                                          CIP

Design by Lee Fukui

Attention: Schools and Businesses

Andrews McMeel books are available at quantity discounts with bulk purchase for educational, business, or sales promotional use. For information, please write to: Special Sales Department, Andrews McMeel Publishing, 4520 Main Street, Kansas City, Missouri 64111.

A heathen approached the sage Rabbi Hillel some two thousand years ago and said that he wanted to convert to Judaism. But the heathen said he was very busy and would consider it only if the Rabbi could teach him everything he needed to know about the religion while the proselyte stood on one foot.

Rabbi Hillel directed the man to stand on one foot.

Said Hillel: "What is hateful to you, do not do to your neighbor. That is the whole of the Torah, the rest is commentary."

Another reflection of this wisdom was presented long ago as the Golden Rule: "Do unto others as you would have them do unto you."

*Do not withhold good
from whom it is due
when it is in your power
to do it.*

PROVERBS

CONTENTS

Introduction

DO THE RIGHT THING

Do unto the other feller
the way he'd like to do unto you
an' do it first.

EDWARD NOYES WESTCOTT
David Harum

Early in the eighteenth century, Israel ben Eliezer, a Polish-born rabbi, became the Baal Shem Tov, the founder of the Chassidic sect of Judaism. For more than 250 years this sect has flourished. I am a direct descendant of the Baal Shem Tov, and all of my forefathers since that time have been ordained as rabbis. I am no exception to this rule.

Although I gave up my pulpit in 1959 to practice psychiatry, the lore, wisdom and ethical beliefs that imbue my family mythology and which formed my growing years have never left me. I am a living link in a chain of wisdom, handed down through folklore, knowledge that is as relevant to the problems we face today as it was centuries ago. The overarching message for all the wisdom and lore in this book is the same: doing good makes us feel good; once we set ourselves on the right path we can't "party" until that favor for a friend is done; it won't feel good.

As much as my family roots begin in the eighteenth century, I am a creature of the twentieth century, with almost forty years' experience as a practicing psychiatrist. In my career as a doctor, I have understood that medicine has its limits, and that ancient wisdom has immeasurable power to heal human hearts. Much of this wisdom promotes the act of kindness as a tool for healing.

As a psychiatrist I specialize in treating addiction. Twenty-five years ago I founded The Gateway Rehabilitation System in Pittsburgh. I am often asked whether any particular treatment modality is employed at Gateway. I always answer that our strength lies in our belief in the inherent goodness of every client. This quality is not always easy to recognize in a person who has led a destructive lifestyle for decades, someone whose use of alcohol or drugs has caused great suffering for others. But in all my years of treating illnesses of the heart and soul, this belief has never failed me: each individual's integrity is always there, lurking right beneath the surface, eager to emerge.

> *Goodness often blossoms like roses on very rickety trellis-work.*
> HUBERT BUTLER, *The Art of the Personal Enemy*

Goodness tends to propagate itself. It's apt to form a chain. A story occurs to me of a man named Avi. I first met him while I was in Tel Aviv speaking before a group of ex-convicts in recovery who were coming into our Israeli rehabilitation program, a sister home to Gateway. When I began to speak of self-esteem, this man interrupted me. "How can you talk to us of this? I've been in and out of jail for half of my thirty-four years. I've been a thief since I was eight. When I'm out of prison I can't find work and my family doesn't want to see me."

I stopped him and asked if he'd passed by a jewelry store lately. "Consider the diamonds in the window," I said.

"Try and think what they look like when they come out of the mine—lumps of dirty ore. It takes a person who understands the diamond to take the shapeless mound and bring out its intrinsic beauty. That's what we do here, we look for the diamond in everyone; we help the soul's beauty come to the surface, we polish it until it gleams." I looked at Avi, all disheveled and hunched over, nearly hiding in his seat, and said, "You're like that dirt-covered ore and our business is to find the diamond within and polish it until it glows."

Two years passed. Avi had graduated from the treatment center, and when the following event took place he had already completed his stay in the halfway house and was integrated into the community, working in construction. One day Annette, who manages the halfway house, received a call from a family whose elderly matriarch had died. They wanted to donate her furniture to the halfway house. Annette called Avi and asked him to pick up the furniture, which he willingly agreed to do. When he went to to pick it up, he saw that it wasn't worth saving but not wanting to insult the family, he hauled it anyway.

While Avi was laboring to carry the shabby sofa up the stairs to the halfway house, an envelope fell from the cushions. After getting the couch inside, Avi retrieved the envelope, in which he found five thousand shekels (about $1,700). Now Avi, remember, had served time in prison for burglary. When he was doing drugs he would have broken into a home for twenty dollars. But now Avi called Annette and told her about the envelope. Annette said it must be reported to the family.

The family was so gratified by Annette's and Avi's honesty that they told her to keep the money for the halfway house. As a result, the halfway house was able to buy one more bed and provide room for one more guest, creating another opportunity for recovery. And Avi wasn't a crook anymore.

Avi relayed this story to me in a letter. He wrote, "When I used drugs I would get a high for a very short time and when the high wore off I felt terrible, worse than before. It's been three months since I found that money and every time I think of what I did, I feel good all over again. How different a feeling than a temporary fix."

Another year went by and I returned to that halfway house where Avi's good deed had set off a chain of events which led to, among other things, an extra bed. There was a sign hanging above the entry. It read: DIAMONDS POLISHED HERE.

Life is what our character makes it.
JULES RENARD, *Journal*

Goodness is inherent in all of us. Sometimes we need the selflessness or charitable behavior of others to bring it to the surface. Or we might need to be reminded of its place right there beneath our skin.

It is no accident that as a society we are experiencing a resurgence of belief in things spiritual. As we approach the new millennium, we instinctively sense that we must turn our priorities around.

Each of us needs an owner's guide to our evolving spirits. The book you hold in your hand didn't get there accidentally. The word "good" in the title attracted you. Already you are partway there. "There" is the place where you will arrive knowing that nothing feels better than performing a kindness for another. Each small good deed builds on the one before until you have a mosaic created from gemstones of kindness. And what will happen while you aren't looking is you'll get so much back in return.

These good deeds you perform are labeled differently in every language: in Yiddish, the word is *mitzvah;* in the United States, it falls under the heading of the Golden Rule. Every culture has an expression for performing an unsolicited good deed for another. Each of these words has the same superlative connotation, suggestive of not only the act of kindness, but the whole spirit surrounding it.

I have been fortunate: through both my pastoral work and the wisdom of my patients, I have learned much about the resources each of us has for goodness and how we must strive to be kind to others in order to love ourselves.

Because I work with addicts I have witnessed countless souls battling their basest demons to gain goodness. Because I am a medical doctor I have watched so often the one-on-one struggle between humankind and illness. And whether the patient wins or loses the struggle, she will always end up changing the lives of everyone around her. When my own tragedies have come, it is the gesture of these same patients, reaching out to share my pain even as they feel their own, that has made my own losses bearable.

This reminds me of a story I read concerning the aftermath of the tragic crash of TWA 800 over Long Island in July 1996. As the victims' families were returning home, unsure of anything, many without even the identification of their loved ones, they were surrounded by strangers wanting to console them. One of the victims' family members stopped to speak to the crowd. She talked of the crowd's tireless support throughout the weeks they had stayed in a makeshift bunker, a hotel. Each morning the bereaved would walk out to signs that read, "We love you," "We pray for you." Individuals in the crowd spoke out their support. The woman wept as she told the press how much this meant to the families. On this particular day, the last of their stay, an impromptu memorial service was held, one of many. The collective sympathy of strangers is an impressive tool to combat grief. Think of that when you know of someone who is grieving. Reach out to them. This is one of so many simple good deeds you can perform—for them; for you.

> *The place to improve the world is first in one's own heart*
> *and head and hands and then work outward from there.*
> ROBERT M. GRSIG, *Zen and the Art of Motorcycle Maintenance*

Storytelling is a way to reach out and touch people's hearts, and unlock the bounty of wisdom which lies inside all of the stories that each of us has to tell about ourselves. When we share our stories with each other, we are building connection, and connection enriches and instructs the soul. As a child, I learned this wisdom by listening to the stories which my father and uncles told stories which I subsequently shared with my own children, and they with theirs. This is how the chain of wisdom remains unbroken: it is through stories that we acquire information to feed our soul. I have known stories to heal. I have known stories to entertain. I have known stories to reach an addict through a miasma of dope and convince him to try and stop. I have known stories to touch people's hearts and help them fall in love.

All of these stories work their magic, but how they work I cannot explain. The mechanics of the power of storytelling cannot, and need not, be articulated. This is a good thing, for like all magic, the healing art of storytelling can be disempowered if one tries to analyze and explain it too closely.

I have seen the power of storytelling take effect many times. A few years ago I began exchanging stories with a friend who had suffered from a terrible cancer that caused him to lose one of his legs. At first, the stories did nothing more than offer him comfort, but just knowing that I had eased his pain made me feel good. As he progressed from hospital to rehabilitation where he struggled with an artificial leg and hip, I continued the habit of calling him. Each morning I would start with a joke, usually a terrible one. And he would rise to the occasion.

Then one night, I dreamed that he and I were dancing, he on his prosthesis, and he was wildly happy, just filled with joy. The next day I shared my dream with him. Soon enough, his nephew was married and my friend did dance at the wedding. In fact we danced together there. Though he is gone now, I would like to believe the sharing of stories and humor helped the quality of his last months.

What follows are stories from across the world—from ancient history to current sources—that recount good deeds and all that can be gained through them. One recurring theme is that the giving of oneself in kindness to another tends to boomerang, bringing the good deed back. It is phrased in Ecclesiastes this way: "Cast your bread upon the waters and eventually it will come back to you." So it is with kindness.

Also these deeds are apt to grow exponentially, forming a wide, all-encompassing arch. And having lived with this subject of The Golden Rule for quite a while I was able to distinguish a pattern. Some acts tend to boost self-esteem, some help one grow spiritually, some expressly bring love, others help break habits. Using prayer or meditation to help another accelerates our own spiritual growth. The very act of replacing toxic thoughts with good deeds toward a possible adversary moves us away from destructive habits such as anger, fear, even addiction. How often has someone made you angry so you lit up a cigarette or took a drink? If you forced yourself to do a kindness for this person, you would change.

For instance: it is told that a spiritual master was repeatedly sought out by a barren woman for a blessing so that she would have a child. One day just as she was leaving the master's abode a man came to ask the spiritual one for a donation so that he could buy a horse. He earned his living by carrying loads for others and his horse had died. He did not have the money to buy another horse and was making all his deliveries by carrying heavy loads on his back. "My back is breaking, sir," he said. "I cannot continue carrying much longer and I must support my family."

The sage called the woman back. "This man has a problem. He is carrying heavy loads. You have a problem in that you have been unable to carry a child. Let us make a switch. You give him some money for a horse so he will no longer have to carry heavy loads and by virtue of this kind deed, you will carry a child." The woman did as she was instructed and soon thereafter was with child.

It is very possible that the positive attitude attendant on the woman's giving charity to the porter was the mechanism which unblocked her reproductive system. Infertility specialists testify to the major psychological component to conception and with all our advancements in the area of fertility, it is more often attitude that can be the determining factor. So this woman freed herself up, perhaps allowed herself to feel worthy, and therefore conceived.

As for the reciprocity of this good deed, maybe not all kindnesses can boomerang so neatly, but more often than not when you are good to another you get whatever you truly need in return.

The eight chapters that follow, each based on a specific tenet, relate to the qualities inherent in giving. Whether a particular deed creates for the doer more self-esteem or promotes a deepening spirituality or any of the eight attributes is important if one seeks to grow in goodness systematically, not leaving this development to chance. My forefathers were very practical about good deeds and believed that one's acts were closely watched and calculated through concrete rules during one's lifetime. This enumeration of good deed "points" is summed up by a story from the Jewish book of knowledge, the Talmud.

A tribunal convened in Heaven to decide the fate of a particular citizen who was, like most of us, sometimes good and sometimes not. The tribunal was arguing whether Mr. Levi's sins should be weighed on the same scale as his good deeds. The angels questioned Mr. Levi very closely: "When you performed the *mitzvah* of giving charity to your fellow townsman anonymously, did you hope that it would multiply?" And Mr. Levi responded that of course, when he gave charity to a family that was starving he hoped that the good deed would have a ripple effect, and so it did, for the once-starving family used their sense of well-being to produce, create a business and make money themselves, which was put back into charity.

"And when you committed the sin of stealing from your neighbor did you hope this transgression would multiply?" asked the angel who communicated the loudest. No, of course not. Mr. Levi said, "When I broke into my neighbor's strongbox I had not the money to feed my children or pay the rent. Certainly I hoped that this deed would not put the other family in a position to create further sin, and in fact, it did not."

The angels decided that Mr. Levi's good deeds would collect interest, thereby adding to to his good deed "account" and burnishing his soul, while the sins would be counted only once, with no "interest."

This tribunal sits in session for all of us, whether we see it as inside ourselves or outside. It's possible to build one's store of good deeds. Ironically it is only possible to do this if we are not "keeping score." How much we actually achieve in concrete terms is not the primary consideration. At the end of the day we will not be judged according to what specific point we have reached but whether we were ascending or descending when our life ended. If we start improving ourselves by doing good for others, we are traveling in a positive direction.

THE EIGHT SPIRITUAL AND PSYCHOLOGICAL TENETS OF THE GOLDEN RULE

One of the kabbalists gives an interesting symbolism to the number eight. Seven, he says, corresponds to a linear progression, like the seven days of the week. For example, if you begin with Sunday, you progress until you reach the last and seventh day, which is Saturday. The eighth day, Sunday, brings you round to the first day. Thus, he says, the number eight symbolizes a return to the beginning.

One might think of the Golden Rule as a purely altruistic principle, which often requires personal sacrifice as we do things for others. The truth is that when we do for others, we are really doing for ourselves, in that we advance in our spirituality, the component that makes us uniquely human and elevates us from all other forms of life.

To be frank, I did not think of this concept when I wrote the eight tenets of the Golden Rule. However, I have long come to believe that there are no coincidences in life, and this is just another example of the purposefulness of unplanned happenings. The eight tenets do indicate the nature of "return to the origin." Thus, the first of these tenets, "It is better to give than to receive," can be understood to mean that receiving is uni-directional, whereas giving is in both directions: he that gives receives.

How wise are the words of the Talmud. "Little does the one who gives alms to the poor realize that the one who receives the alms is actually doing more for the donor than the donor is doing for the recipient." When I eat bread, I have but a single pleasure, in that I satiate my hunger. When I give of my bread to the hungry, my pleasure is doubled. Long after my appetite has been satiated, I can enjoy having provided relief to another person's distress.

There are thus eight principles of spirituality.

Chapter One

IT IS BETTER TO GIVE
THAN TO RECEIVE

*To give and then not feel that one has given
is the very best of all ways of giving.*

MAX BEERBOHM
Hosts and Guests

Yossi's Heart

Yossi was born with a defective heart. His parents were advised that he would need an operation when he turned seven and that the operation was best done in America.

Yossi's parents, both Israelis, knew no one in America, so when the time came a mutual friend put them in touch with me and I found a medical center in Pittsburgh, where I live, where the surgery could be performed. Several months later Yossi and his parents arrived.

Neither Yossi nor his parents understood a single word of English so I put out the word in the Pittsburgh community for anyone who spoke Hebrew to contact me. Twenty-nine people volunteered and I contacted all of them for an emergency meeting.

At this meeting I explained the predicament. Yossi would be hospitalized for at least two weeks and it was absolutely essential that an interpreter be available at all times. There was no way he could make himself understood to the staff. I asked people to volunteer several hours of their time to be in attendance and we arranged a schedule that covered twenty-four hours a day for two weeks. Each person had an assigned time, and we agreed that one person would not leave until the next arrived.

The plan operated like clockwork. Yossi and his parents were never left alone and not only was there effective interpretation, but the family also received the support of interested people. The postoperative period was not without many anxious moments and Yossi's parents swear that without the moral support of so many friends, they could never have survived it.

The entire hospital staff was impressed by this community cooperation and devotion and when Yossi was discharged the surgeon waived his bill! The family had no insurance coverage and the hospital wrote off whatever they could and gave them the lowest rate. This was paid through donations made by friends of the small community that had sprung up around Yossi.

Before Yossi left for home a gala party was held, attended by the volunteers, contributors, surgeon and other members of the hospital staff. Tearful good-byes were said, there was much embracing, lots of people gave of themselves and got back this: they had helped save a little boy. Along the way each one discovered qualities inside that might never have been tapped if not for Yossi. On top of this many friendships had been formed during this period and these people who had not known each other became close friends, having worked for a common cause.

Six years later on a visit to Israel I made a surprise visit to Yossi, but he wasn't home: he was playing basketball! I went to the playground and could not stop my tears of joy when I saw the robust little boy who had once been so hampered by illness playing a game of hoops. On my return to Pittsburgh I contacted the participants in Yossi's operation for a reunion and we all bonded again as we shared the news. One man originally had been reluctant to help because he was terrified of hospitals. Now he relayed that he no longer hesitated to visit friends when they were ill; he had gotten over a phobia that had controlled him.

It's twenty years later. Yossi is happily married and has a child. He sends cards twice a year which we circulate. In this way the group stays in touch and when a member needs help or wants to share happiness we are there.

What we did for Yossi pales in comparison to what Yossi did for us. Each of us is stronger as a result of this event. That is the power of goodness.

The Rabbi's Gift

A recent theory regarding chaos suggests that the mere flapping of a butterfly's wings in the air over, let us say Mexico, creates a current which ripples around the world to touch the tides of oceans in, say, Australia. The more I think about this the more I want to live my life by the Golden Rule. It says to me that each of our deeds, even those as small as the flapping of a butterfly's wings, has great consequences for now and who knows how many eons to follow. Perhaps the man in this story knew about this theory—more likely he was a natural at following the Golden Rule.

Some years ago a renowned scholar named Rabbi Akiva Eger had a number of guests for his Passover Seder. One guest accidentally tipped over his goblet of wine. To prevent his being embarrassed Rabbi Eger promptly nudged the leg of the table with his knee causing several other goblets to spill and giving the impression that it was the table's shakiness, not his guest's clumsiness, which caused the spill.

The rabbi exhibited here the epitome of character refinement. His instinctive response shows to what level a person can rise by acting frequently out of kindness, by being as concerned about another's dignity as one's own. The habit of giving is etched so deeply inside Rabbi Eger that he goes directly to the good deed he might extend.

The Mill Owner
Who Wove a Good Deed

This man, one closer to home, whose story is told below, also instinctively gives to others, not thinking at all of what he might receive in return.

I must start by saying this story came to me in a circuitous way, without my searching for it, which is typical of this particular good deed story. This is a *mitzvah* that happened without the giver talking about it. It is about goodness that happened and then continued to flourish.

In Lexington, Massachusetts, December 1995, a wind-blown fire destroyed the Malden Mills, effectively stealing away Christmas from its fourteen hundred workers. For Lexington, Malden was the only game in town and had been for a number of generations. There were many who were certain the mill's owner, seventy-year-old Aaron Feuerstein, would simply retire and close the mill down. But that wasn't

what Feuerstein had in mind when he met with his workers
four days after the fire.

Aaron Feuerstein searched his soul, and remembered a
lesson his father had taught him. "In a situation," Feuerstein
quoted Hillel, "which is devoid of morality, try to be
thoughtful and do something worthwhile." The mill owner
decided to keep all his employees on full payroll, with bene-
fits, for at least a month, during which time he made arrangements for a hasty reopening of the mill. This large-scale good
deed quickly spread, much like the fire that had prompted it,
and it sparked a remarkable surge of goodwill. Donations
soon poured in from people all over the country, including
toys for the children, frozen turkeys for Christmas dinner,
even tickets to performances of the Nutcracker Suite in
nearby Boston.

What the mill families received is quantifiable. For Mr.
Feuerstein, this action did much more than just "accrue"
goodness to his soul. It connected him in a deeper way to his
fourteen hundred workers. "When I give I give myself,"
wrote Walt Whitman. Mr. Feuerstein has more than resolved
whatever issues we all have concerning our capacity for
goodness.

The mill was reopened in record time. Further, Mr.
Feuerstein was invited as an honored guest to President
Clinton's 1996 State of the Union address, a singular honor
offered in recognition of great Americans.

Danny Thomas's Mitzvah Story

The following true tale comes out of my own life stories.

When I decided to go to medical school I was married with two children and a third on the way. I held a low-paying position as an assistant rabbi and my father helped support me and my family.

The tuition for medical school was formidable but I was able to manage for a while, using donations from my congregation and some loans. But by the middle of my third year, I was in debt up to my ears and unable to go on. I wrote to foundations that gave scholarships to medical students, but I was turned down. What to do?

I usually called home during the day to see how my wife was feeling and one day she said, "What would you do if you had four thousand dollars?"

"I'd travel around the world." Can't she see I'm busy, I said to myself. "I have no time for daydreaming," is what I said aloud.

"This is not a daydream. There is a check for four thousand dollars on its way to you."

"Did you forge it?"

"No, Danny Thomas is giving you four thousand dollars."

I had no idea who Danny Thomas was and wondered if perhaps my wife's pregnancy was making her a little strange. But after we'd gone back and forth about this check, she read to me the following story out of the *Chicago Sun-Times*.

At a meeting with officials from Marquette University, the officials told Danny Thomas about the plight of a young rabbi who was having a difficult time financing his education. "How much does the rabbi need?" Danny Thomas asked. "About four thousand dollars," the Marquette officials said. "Tell your rabbi he's got it." Like it happened all the time, I thought. But sure enough several days later I received a call from Danny Thomas who affirmed that the money was coming in a few days.

For the rest of Danny Thomas's life, we were in touch. I have no idea what Danny received spiritually from his generosity to strangers. I do know that I received a medical degree as well as confirmation of my belief and pride in humankind.

One material return Danny Thomas received came about many years later and I am forever grateful for having been a part of it.

Danny traveled around the country raising money for the hospital he had built that specialized in leukemia, the Shrine of St. Jude. He came to Milwaukee to raise money and

I contacted people on his behalf asking that they attend a fund-raising dinner.

That evening I was given the opportunity to make a presentation to Danny Thomas of the pledges we had raised for the charity which meant so much to him. At this time I shared with everyone what Danny had done for me. I was embarrassed by my tearfulness and avoided looking out at the group. But finally as I presented Danny with a gift, I had to look up and that's when I found many of those in the room weeping the same tears of gratitude and admiration for this great, kind man. I also gave him a beautiful volume of the Bible with a silver filigree cover inscribed with this verse from Micah: "For what does the Lord God ask of you, but to act with kindness, do justice and walk humbly with your God."

Mitzvahs not only bind but also break through barriers, bringing people together as the brothers they should be. Who would think of a less likely combination: a Lebanese Christian and a Chassidic rabbi?

A father rejoices when he sees his children acting kindly to each other. Danny and I certainly took pleasure in what we had done for each other, and since we had done what God asks of us, our pleasure was increased manifold by our awareness that we had made our Father happy as well.

No Good Deed Comes Undone

No good deed we have done can be taken away from us.

During the early fifteenth century, the golden era of Jews in Spain, Don Isaac Abravanel was an adviser to the king. Some who were envious of his success tried to impugn him by telling the king that Don Isaac had prospered by embezzling from the royal treasury. Although the king did not believe this, his suspicions were sufficiently aroused for him to ask Don Isaac to provide him with an accurate accounting of all he owned.

Several days later Don Isaac gave the king a list which amounted to a relatively small sum. "This is hardly a tenth of what I know you own."

Don Isaac responded, "When your Majesty asked me for an accounting of my possessions I knew it was because some of my enemies have been maligning me. If they succeed then your Majesty will confiscate everything I have. Thus, these are hardly things I possess because I can lose them in just a moment. I therefore made a calculation of whatever money I have given to charity, because that can never be confiscated from me, and what I have given away is truly the only thing I can say that I own."

A Payback—Not a Sacrifice

When we opened Gateway in 1972 we were promised that medical insurance would pay for our clients' treatment by April of that year. We did not receive payments until August of 1975. We received meager payment for some clients from the state and even that was often delayed. I kept Gateway open by soliciting funds from various donors.

One day our administrator, Sister Germaine, called me. "We can't meet next week's payroll."

I said, "Sister, I have exhausted all my sources. I can't go back for more."

"What will we do?" Sister asked.

"If we close, we will do it next Thursday (payday), not before. We teach our clients to live one day at a time, so we must too."

Thursday came and went. We did not close down, and I did not ask how or why.

Ten years later I learned that our accountant, Ed, a man of sixty-six, had taken a mortgage on his home to make the payroll. Given our precarious circumstances, there was no reason for Ed to think he would ever be repaid (thank God he was).

Oh, by the way, many years earlier Ed had been helped to overcome his alcohol addiction, so for him this deed was like repaying a favor rather than a potential sacrifice of a huge sum of money.

With devotion like this, it is little wonder why Gateway has been able to help so many people. And with people like Ed in the world, there is no reason we all can't help and be helped whenever there is trouble or pain.

The Giving—Taking Circle

A woman I'll call Bonnie, a member of our program, was in her first year of sobriety when she confided to a mutual friend that she had slept for three winter nights in an unheated apartment. There had been an extended frigid spell and her furnace broke down. Because there was a backlog of calls for service, the repairman was unable to get to her home for four days. Our mutual friend said, "How silly of you. You could have called me or any of your friends and stayed with us." Bonnie responded, "I don't like to impose."

When this was related to me, I called Bonnie and told her that I was disappointed because I had hoped to be able to call on her to help newcomers in the twelve-step program she frequented adjust to their struggle. Bonnie was nonplussed, "You can call on me anytime, doctor. I'll be glad to help."

"No, I cannot," I said. "If you cannot accept help, you cannot give it either."

The Miser's Golden Rule

In the city of Berdichev there lived a wealthy man, named Isaac Boruchovich, who had a reputation for being a miser. Berdichev was the commercial center for the many small villages and towns in the surrounding countryside. Since travel in those days was cumbersome and time-consuming, merchants in the smaller communities would designate a person to do all their purchasing for them. Essentially, they would give him a shopping list and money, and he would bring them all the merchandise they desired from Berdichev.

One day such a purchasing agent, while making a transaction, discovered that his money belt was missing. The awareness that he had lost such a vast sum, for which he was personally liable and which he could not possibly pay back, was more than he could bear, and he fainted, not once, but repeatedly. As soon as he would come to he would recall his misfortune all over again, and set to wailing until he fainted.

As Boruchovich was crossing through the square, he noticed the crowd that had gathered. Curious to know what had happened, he approached the crowd and asked what was going on. Upon being informed, he pushed his way through to the center, and the next time the man came to, he shouted: "Don't worry, my friend. Your money belt is safe."

Needless to say the purchasing agent remained conscious.

"Now listen," Boruchovich continued, "I have found a money belt, and in all likelihood it is the one you lost. But obviously you must give me adequate identification so that I know I am returning it to its true owner."

The man then proceeded to describe the belt. "Yes," said Boruchovich. "But that is a standard type of money belt. Can you give me more precise identification, such as how much money it contained and in what denominations?"

Without delay the man promptly reported the exact number of bills, and in what denominations. Boruchovich then said, "I will be home in about an hour. You should come see me at that time. If the contents of the belt correspond to the amounts you enumerated, I will gladly return it to you."

Boruchovich then hurried away down a side street and made his way to a store, where he purchased a money belt such as the man had described. He then rushed home and filled it with the correct number of bills, in the correct denominations. When the man arrived shortly thereafter, Boruchovich informed him that the money in the belt indeed corresponded with his account, and turned the belt over to him.

The man was so elated to have been saved from financial ruin that in his euphoria he failed to notice that the belt was brand-new, whereas the belt he had lost was well-worn.

Word of the incident meanwhile spread through Berdichev, and the person who had in truth found and kept the lost money belt was plagued by remorse. How could he keep this money when a total stranger had given such a vast sum of his own to save the man's sanity? This tormenting question gave him no peace, until he finally took the money belt and sought out its owner. When he had found the purchasing agent, he confessed what had happened and surrendered the money belt to him.

The purchasing agent immediately noted that this old, worn money belt was indeed his, and that Boruchovich's belt was a new one. After thanking the finder, he made his way to Boruchovich and offered to return the latter's money. But surprisingly Boruchovich refused to accept the money! "God provided me with an opportunity for a *mitzvah*," he said, "and I do not want to undo it. Return the lost belt to the person who found it," he continued, "he may have need of it." The finder, however, was equally adamant that after his weakness in yielding to temptation, he did not wish to be unjustly enriched, and therefore refused to accept the money. Ultimately Boruchovich and the agent both got their money back. And though Boruchovich had been at one time a miser, by the end of his life he had given so much to others that his character was thoroughly changed.

The Snowball Effect

My doctor has convinced me that it is time I use a snowblower rather than a shovel, and this gave me an opportunity to test the tenet It Is Better to Give Than to Receive:

The blizzard of '94 was a record-breaker in the northeast and I was happy to have a chance to use my new toy. I have a rather long driveway, so clearing it took time. Then, since I was already out there I cleared the drives for both my neighbors, one to the right and one to the left. I felt terrific. I had good exercise, was thinking nice thoughts, felt happy to have done a good deed. These pleasures were reward enough for my work. Yet there was another reward: soon after clearing the snow I received a letter from a charity close to my heart that reported a contribution had been made in my name. The accompanying note read:

"To Dr. Twerski: In appreciation of your shoveling our sidewalk! Your neighbors."

Do It Because You Have to and Then Do It Because You Want To

A beggar sat at the wall of the city. When a scholar walked past he placed two alms in the beggar's box and walked on. A few minutes later the same scholar returned and again placed two alms in the beggar's box.

"Why are you giving to me twice?" he asked.

The scholar said, "Because the first time I gave alms for me. Now I give them for you."

The issue of which is superior, being driven to give out of emotion versus out of obligation, is an important point for those of us in the "business" of religion. Jews, as an example, are instructed by the Talmud that the reward for performing an act of kindness when commanded is higher than if one acts from the heart. Psychologically, the masters believed that since one had to overcome resistance to follow a command, she or he should receive greater recognition, at least by God.

Humans are creatures of habit: the more we repeat certain acts, the more they become integrated into our personalities. If you find you have difficulty in doing something desirable, you need to practice it but a few times to overcome the resistance. We may feel some resistance if we are called upon to extend ourselves for others, since this may be an imposition on our comfort. It is therefore wise to volunteer our efforts, and as we develop a habit of doing things for others, it will be only natural to respond to a request or even a command to be of help.

The Joy of Giving

One of my favorite little stories explains it this way:

A young couple of my acquaintance were to be married and invited me to the opulent affair. In truth, I worried over this event, not wanting to hurt either the couple or the parents, all four of whom had been in my congregation so many years before. But the wedding was so, well, lavish and expensive—what other words can I use—that I thought how wasteful it would prove to be when so many others are needy. How could I partake in such an event? How could I give my heart to it and truly wish them well?

An idea, a very obvious one actually, came to me that I knew would satisfy my dilemma. I requested that the couple give the leftover food to an operation in Milwaukee that arranges to remove such leftovers and distribute them to the needy. To my great delight, the couple had already arranged this and indeed many of their friends in their "social set" often donated leftovers in this way.

The next idea came from Ida, a woman who attended my wife when my daughter was born. She suggested that the flowers be donated at the end of the evening to Mt. Sinai Hospital where she worked as a nurse. Actually, it seemed like such a great idea that I wanted some of those flowers to be donated to a local psychiatric hospital where many of the patients never receive flowers.

The couple loved this idea. I danced and celebrated at the wedding, and early in the morning, thirty medical students from Marquette University came to get the flowers and distribute them. A week later I received a thank-you note from the newlyweds. They wrote that the fact that the flowers and food brought cheer to those less fortunate was a great way to start their new life, and a good omen for a happy marriage.

Just recently I had the opportunity for a repeat performance. I attended a wedding which had many floral arrangements and my suggestion to donate the flowers to the St. Francis Hospital Alcoholism Unit where many Gateway patients began their journey to recovery was readily accepted.

Now, I suppose I could have looked at the lavish spreads and beautiful flowers at both of these affairs as well as the happy couples who made me think of my dear Goldie, recently passed away, and been envious of people who had each other, who could spend money so freely. But that would only have given me a gnawing feeling in my stomach that would signal that my "bones were rotting" with envy. Surely a bad sign. Instead there were *mitzvahs* galore. Those who owned the flowers had a *mitzvah*. Same with the food. Those who distributed the food and the students who distributed the flowers all had *mitzvahs*. I had one. Sister Adele, the CEO of St. Francis Hospital, who will one day be canonized as the saintly person she was, did too. And a young couple felt they had started their lives off on the right foot. "Man discovers his own wealth when God comes to ask gifts of him," wrote Rabindranath Tagore. How wonderful to give! And how wonderful to know that when we give we develop the quality to be able to give more easily, even when it may be an imposition on our comfort.

The Subject of Angels

Early in this century in an affluent community in Poland the local hospital had deteriorated and the citizens were derelict about refurbishing it. When the holy sage, referred to as the Chofetz Chaim (which loosely translates to one who truly loves life and shows great respect for His Holiness), visited the town and saw what was happening to the poor, he called a meeting of the community's more affluent citizens.

"In the community of Biala," he told them, "there was at one point no medical facility and the poor who became ill were cared for at home whereas the wealthy could travel to larger cities for hospital care.

"As we know, God sends angels to look after the sick and the angels began complaining to God: why is He always sending them to such uninviting surroundings—shabby, unheated, etc. Why doesn't He send them more often to nicer surroundings, the angels wanted to know.

"The angels' complaint was heeded and God began causing more of the wealthy people to become sick. Not all of them were in shape to travel so they remained in their homes and the angels were pleased to be in such lavish accommodations.

"The wealthy, realizing what was happening, quickly built a comfortable well-furnished hospital which was available for the poor, so that the angels would not complain. Indeed, the wealthy stopped getting so sick.

"Now in your community," the Chofetz Chaim said, "the hospital has deteriorated to shabby conditions, very unpleasant for the angels. It is inevitable that they will complain again. So if you wish to preserve your health, I suggest you contribute to refurbishing the hospital."

When we give for others, we are helping ourselves.

An "Unrude" Awakening

Clancy is a recovering alcoholic with more than forty years' sobriety. He has sponsored hundreds of "pigeons" as he calls them, helping them win the battle. Anytime one of his pigeons takes a drink or is about to he or she calls Clancy. Frequently this happens in the middle of the night.

"Doesn't it bother you when you are awoke so often?" someone asked.

"Hell no," he said. "I'm grateful I'm not the one that's doing the calling."

No wonder AA emphasizes spiritual awakening, it now occurs to me. Even a "rude" alarm in the early hours can be spiritual when one is aware she is helping others.

Chapter Two

GOOD DEEDS CREATE CONNECTIONS

There is no hope of joy except in human relations.

ANTOINE DE SAINT-EXUPÉRY
Flight to Arras

The Yiddish word for a good deed is *mitzvah,* as in, "Harry takes Mrs. Solomon every day to the park. This is some *mitzvah!"* The denotation is good deed, but the connotation is much larger; it is the milieu and the spirit accompanying the performance of the deed. The same holds true for Hillel's direction to the convert, which is the epigraph to this book, as well as for the Golden Rule.

The second meaning of *mitzvah* is connection. That stands to reason. When we show kindness to another a bridge is built between us and them. Follow the Golden Rule to its logical conclusion and you will have formed relations with the many people for whom you harbor good feelings. The selfish life is one that pampers only the body; the spiritual life emphasizes expression of the soul. When we do for others we are setting aside ourselves, which is a spiritual deed. Good deeds therefore help dissolve the barrier between one person and another and allow us to briefly become one.

Some people seek ways in which to become one with the universe, which can be achieved through meditation or, if one wishes to be delusional, through the ingestion of chemicals. A far greater achievement is to become one with others. The optimal way to accomplish this is through *mitzvah.*

We're All Connected

The following story is true, for I witnessed it with my own eyes. It forever convinced me how important it is for human beings to connect, no matter how "far gone" we might think they are. Humans need to reach each other.

Early in my career I served as a psychiatrist in a large state hospital where there were hundreds of mentally ill patients, some of whom had been there for many years. Medical students would visit the hospital periodically and I would tour the facility with them, pointing out "museum pieces," i.e., cases that are described in psychiatric literature but rarely encountered outside of an institution.

On touring a chronic care building I pointed out a man who was the most "senior" patient in the hospital. He had been admitted fifty-two years earlier at the age of seventeen with the diagnosis "dementia praecox," because the term schizophrenia had not yet been coined. This man was mute, his records showing that he had not spoken a single word in fifty-two years.

The patient had a routine whereby following breakfast he would go to a corner of the community room and assume an absurd contorted position with his hands directed upward, and he would maintain this position for hours until he was called to lunch. Following lunch he would return to this position until supper, and thereafter until bedtime. Neither talk therapy nor medications nor electroshock treatment had served to alter this behavior, which he had maintained all these years. No amount of urging could get him to sit down except at mealtime and he often developed edema of his feet as a result of his immobility and his posture.

On one of the medical students' visits one young man asked if he could talk to the patient. "Certainly," I said, wondering what impact he thought he could make on this patient when decades of psychiatric efforts had failed.

The student approached the patient and said, "You must be tired. Go sit down." The man gave him a blank stare and did not move. The student then assumed the contorted position of the patient, equaling his posture with great precision, and then said, "I'll stand here like this. You can go sit down." Without a word, the patient sat down on a bench for the first time in fifty-two years!

While it is impossible to know what was going on in this man's mind, it is likely that his delusion may have been that by assuming this particular position, he was holding up the universe, and he clearly could not submit to all entreaties to leave that position, lest the world collapse. (You may ask, as we all did, why did he leave to eat and sleep? But there was no rationale to this behavior.)

For all those years no one had understood this person until this ingenious medical student solved the mystery. But why? Granted this was irrational behavior but what we suddenly understood was that this unusual behavior had great meaning to the patient, but no one had tried to understand it. The strange behavior was just dismissed as "crazy" and no more consideration was given it or him. But by showing this patient compassion and understanding, the medical student gained a *mitzvah*, he showed kindness and allowed the patient to feel some relief. Further, a connection was formed between the irrational mind and the rational. Who knows how far such an understanding might have gone if it had happened many years before.

Understanding another no matter how far apart our beliefs might be is a *mitzvah* in both senses of the word—a kindness, a connection. If more often more of us tried to build this bridge there's no telling where such kindness might take us. Think about it the next time someone around you acts in a way you can't immediately understand.

Dotty Lived and Died by the Golden Rule

Dotty was a woman who came to Gateway for treatment at the age of forty-six. How she had survived until that age is a mystery because she had begun abusing substances at the age of fourteen and in the years that followed she had countless brushes with accidental death from overdose. Once she achieved sobriety she threw herself wholeheartedly into trying to help others recover and many people owe their lives to Dotty.

Still, she never shook off entirely the wounds and fears from her drugging days. Once we attended a funeral of a mutual friend together and we were two out of ten mourners in attendance. When we left the cemetery Dotty said to me, "When I die, I want there to be a procession two miles long because I want to have made the friends I could not make when I was drugging."

At age sixty-two Dotty was diagnosed with cancer. Her hospital room was always busy with the noise of friends visiting and trying their best to be there for her. Many of these were friends she had helped recover; some she'd pulled back from the brink of death. To say they were all connected is a compliment to Dotty on a life lived to great purpose.

When Dotty died, she indeed had a long funeral procession and if it was not a full two miles long, it was not much less.

During her early life, Dotty was very much alone, disconnected. You can't relate when your mind is in a state of suspended animation. Once she recovered, Dotty loved and was loved. She was not alone in life nor abandoned in death. Her helping others, her good deeds, gained her connection.

Connection—Nine Letters
That Go Horizontal and Vertical

"It's important to connect one's life with the larger whole. Without integration there is no meaning; with no meaning there is despair."

Psychologist Dr. Mary Pipher wrote this in her book, *The Shelter of Each Other: Rebuilding Our Families.*

In the course of her work with families, the doctor had cause to examine her grandparents, named Page, who raised their children in Colorado in the 1930s—not an easy existence. But because of the struggle, Dr. Pipher recounts, the Page family and its place in the community was cohesive. In other words, they were connected to each other and to those outside, which translated into the need to care for all of those in this circle, to do good for each other. The doctor concludes that the stories we hear of communities pulling together in times of disaster must be extended so that we pull together in all times. This book so affected one reviewer, Bruce Scheider, that he tells this story:

He was moved enough to travel to visit his deceased mother's last living siblings. He easily picked up his relationship with these relatives, reclaiming his childhood times spent passing the time in their homes and, as he says, "opening my heart to a love that is deeper than I realized." Mr. Schneider leaves us with the image of his eighty-seven-year-old uncle whom he hadn't seen in ten years, slowly moving toward him, open-armed, in the nursing home where he now lived. Mr. Schneider's need to connect, sparked by Dr. Pipher's need to encourage, has, he says unequivocally, "taught me to hold people with more acceptance and forgiveness." He then went on to share this experience with his own children who gained more connection to the family.

And that is how community legends originate; if only we can live their truths.

Heal the Healer

There are all kinds of giving, gifts of money and necessities, and then there is support and a piece of oneself.

Many years ago a young woman I'll call Robin was admitted to Gateway out of prison where she was jailed for repeatedly committing crimes to support her narcotics habit, some of those crimes fairly ugly. Her therapist at the center took great interest in her and told me that it was imperative we find a long-term facility for Robin rather than sending her back out on the street. She was certain that if Robin was released from our relatively short program that she would relapse, violate her probation, and end up once again in prison.

I found a program for Robin which could provide residential treatment for a year. However Robin refused to hear of it.

We periodically hold meetings with staff and patients where we gather to discuss various issues and air grievances. At one such meeting, with Robin in attendance, the director threw the room open to anyone who had something to share. After some silence, Robin's therapist blurted out that she was going to quit. She began to cry. She went on to say that she had put her guts into Robin and she was positive Robin would not stay clean if she left treatment. Rather than watch her patient destroy herself, the therapist was determined to quit.

At this point Robin rose, walked across the room and put her arm around her therapist whose despondency persisted. Many of the patients and staff members tried to cajole her into going on for more treatment but Robin remained adamant. It was quite a role reversal with the therapist crying and Robin comforting her.

A few days later the therapist found me in my office and said, "Something about Robin has changed. I think she can make it on her own as an outpatient after all." Indeed, Robin left the facility, attended recovery meetings and remained out of jail.

I wondered just what had worked for Robin and at a recovery meeting I heard her tell her story: she had been raised in several foster homes. "No one had ever really cared for me," she said. "I got to feel useless, a burden to everyone. I hated the world for treating me like a worthless piece of junk.

"I didn't believe anyone could care for me. When my therapist cried over my refusal to go for long-term treatment, worrying about what might happen to me, it was the first time in my life that anyone ever really cared about what might happen to me. I couldn't believe her feelings were for real and for a while I continued to test her sincerity. When I realized her caring was genuine it gave me hope that maybe the world was not as cruel or uncaring as I thought."

Robin's therapist cared for her—and not only within the artifice of the therapist-patient connection. Caring for another is a gift, showing that feeling is a good deed. The connection that results from this sharing of feeling forms an unbreakable bond. Caring starts with just one hand put out there toward another. It's an antidote to isolation and brings as much spiritual joy to the "carer" as it does to the "caree."

Crisis Means Opportunity—
And the Chance to Connect

While I was still a practicing rabbi I received an emergency call that taught me in five short days the value of connecting to another.

A couple I knew had six children, the youngest a little girl. The family lived near a lake and the baby daughter was warned never to go to the lake alone. One afternoon the little one failed to respond to her mother's calls and shouts. Frantically, the mother, Eve, looked all over the house and the yard, everywhere she could think to look but the lake. Horrible to say, the baby was finally discovered drowned.

Eve could not forgive herself and could not be consoled. I had been called to offer counsel and to perform the service. After the service, I paid a visit on the family as they sat shiva (the week of mourning following a burial). After a while one person bid Eve and her husband good-bye and left. Then another left. Then two, three, more, and so on. Finally only

Eve, her family, and myself remained. Then the family left, except for Eve's husband. That is when Eve began to cry. As she sobbed she asked me why God had taken her baby and why oh why she had been so negligent—perhaps if she'd looked at the lake immediately the baby would have been saved.

I did not attempt to answer her questions. What was there to say? I simply stayed by her side and listened patiently until her tears abated.

The next day this same scene was repeated all over again and it was the same story until four days had passed. Each day after all of her relatives had left me alone with Eve and her husband she cried and bewailed her negligence. On the fifth day her in-laws called to thank me for all I had done for Eve. What had I done? I had barely managed to say anything intelligent because I was rendered so powerless in the face of her grief. But then I realized that the family was too close to Eve's grief to talk to her and for this reason she had no one to "unload" with but me. She was grieved twice: first by the terrible death of her daughter and again by the isolation inadvertently imposed on her by her friends and relatives. And from this experience I gained a valuable insight about connecting. We should never leave the grieving alone nor isolate the sick because of fear.

Now I always counsel friends of those in mourning to stay close. Sit. Listen. Allow your presence to be felt. Sometimes that is the greatest gift we can give to another person—just connecting in silence—just being there.

Change Changes Us

Good deeds really do have the power to change us. I have seen it happen. But I didn't always understand this simple truth until many years ago, when I received a call from the hospital where I was serving my internship.

While I was in medical school I continued to function as a rabbi, and in my fourth year the hospital called saying that someone was requesting a rabbi. When I responded to the call I met a distraught young mother standing over the oxygenated crib of her two-week-old infant. The baby had been born with what was then an inoperable heart defect and could not survive more than a few days. The woman looked up at me with tearful eyes and asked, "Why, Rabbi, Why?"

I felt so helpless, so inadequate, perhaps even more intensely so because I was now representing the two major helping professions, medicine and religion, and neither one, not even both combined, could provide any help. I stayed by her side, said a prayer, then remained a bit longer in silence because I had nothing to say.

The following morning I reported the incident to my father and told him how frustrated I had felt. I could not understand why God allowed such things to happen. It all seemed so futile.

"Look at it this way," my father said, "That woman is not the same person she was before all this happened, and because you tried but failed to console her you are not the same person you were yesterday. Since you both have undergone changes, the incident has moved you. We should never consider any act that changes us as futile."

I took these words to heart and from that point on I visited the infant's mother for I knew what time she appeared at the nursery and I was there when the baby died. For the week or two we spent by the glass wall looking in at the baby we talked, shared experiences; we passed the time that was agonizing for her. A number of times she mentioned how good it was of me to come, she wasn't even Jewish, but ironically it was I who wanted to thank her. She had given me the material with which to dig down deep and to plant strong bulbs in myself that would fortify me to be there for my patients when I couldn't change a thing, just go through their suffering with them.

Conceived in Hate;
Blooms into Kindness

Newton Township in Pennsylvania is a toddler of a community, formed four years ago. For Hanukkah, 1996, one resident placed her electric menorah in her window, as always, when Hanukkah began. She thought nothing about it until she and her husband were awakened to the sound of breaking glass. Vandals had smashed the window to get at the menorah, which they then destroyed.

Word spread quickly through this community in Bucks County. The neighbors (of all religions) were horrified, but didn't know what to do. Then they hit on the idea of putting menorahs in all their windows, sort of like the hero in a story standing in front of the helpless and saying, "You'll have to come through me first!"

At first only a few were involved. But then it just grew. One neighbor, Mrs. Dearing (not her real name) went to the Thrift Drug store and explained her story to the pharmacist, who determined that there were six electric menorahs available in the area. Mrs. Dearing kept looking and finally distributed eighteen menorahs in the neighborhood. By the end of the day eighteen homes on the street where this occurred had menorahs in their windows on this last night of Hanukkah.

While putting away her new electric menorah, Mrs. Dearing said: "I will display it for the rest of my life." Another said she had seen the devastation and pain in the faces of the couple before the *mitzvah* of their neighbors.

One can only imagine how good the victims feel; instead of the sting of hatred they are left with the stroke of love.

Me and Cecilia

This story makes me very sad.

When I entered my psychiatric training one of my first patients was a sixteen-year-old girl who had been hospitalized for depression and a school phobia. I was assigned a supervisor who was a psychiatrist in private practice and he told me that no treatment would be of avail as long as the young woman avoided school. He further said that she must go to school by hook or crook. "I am an aggressive therapist," this doctor said. "I personally pick up my school phobic patients and drive them to school."

This sounded like a good idea so I told my patient, Cecilia, that I would expect her to be standing on the hospital steps the next morning and that I would drive her to school. Indeed she was there at 8:00 A.M. the next day and I drove her to school that day and the following two as well. On the way to school we had the chance to talk not as therapist to patient but as two human beings who had respect for each other.

The third day I was called to the medical director's office. "Dr. Twerski," he said, "I hear that you have been driving Cecilia to school."

"Yes," I said, "Dr. Roberts suggested I do this."

"I understand," the medical director said, "but Dr. Roberts is in private practice and he may do as he wishes. But you must understand, Dr. Twerski, that I cannot permit a young resident to take a female patient in his car. While I certainly can trust you, I cannot say the same for all the other young men on the staff. I cannot say 'yes' to you and 'no' to someone else. So please explain to Cecilia why you can no longer drive her to school."

I met with Cecilia that day and explained the problem to her and she appeared to understand. "But that doesn't change things," I reassured her, "I expect you to go to school tomorrow and I will be here to meet with you on your return."

The next morning at 11:00 A.M. I received a call to come to the medical director's office. On her way to school, Cecilia had jumped off a bridge and killed herself. The medical director had received the news from the homicide squad.

I was as devastated as if I were standing at ground zero at Hiroshima. I began to cry. "Homicide squad," I said. "That's exactly what it was, not a suicide, a homicide."

While the medical director tried to comfort me, there was no place for logic in my feelings. This young child had been placed in my care and I felt responsible for her. She was dead at age sixteen and I had failed her. That was all there was to it.

This event occurred December 2, 1960. For many years after, long after I was out of training I would call the medical director to ask him something and a day or two later it would occur to me that it was invariably the first of week of December. I never planned this, but my unconscious was putting me in touch with the only source of comfort available. I don't know what would have happened to me had I not had this wonderful mentor. When he smoked himself to death, I am ashamed to say I was angry and though he had been such a comfort to me, I did not attend his funeral. I felt he had purposely broken off our connection, just as I felt I had severed my connection to Cecilia. And each early December, I go into a funk and survive partly because someone cared about me and helped pull me through and now I must do the same for myself.

Connections between people grow deep very quickly. When you give to someone you have made an investment in another human being. Part of yourself is now bound to that person and like any other investment you will naturally wish to protect it, just as you will want to protect that part of yourself now within the other. As the Chinese proverb goes, if you save a man you own his soul forever. So it is with *mitzvah,* good deed. It's essential to be mindful of the impact our kindness toward another can have. While I cannot blame myself for what happened to Cecilia I know always that I reached her, and then, in my eyes, if not hers, failed her. And it's a memory that will never let go.

Safety Net

The greatest good deed is to save the life of another person and while some people discredit the concept that prayer for another can help save that person, the validity of this phenomenon has been proved. The healing effects of prayer have been demonstrated even in situations where the patient does not know that others pray for him or her. It is no longer unscientific to assume that there are extrasensory factors constantly at work and that praying for another might tap into that person's body/mind to help them heal.

Good deeds connect us and the kindness of praying for someone's recovery is a connection to that person, even if he or she is a stranger. Prayer can be a major support for someone who needs help and, in fact, might be effective where science fails.

When I applied for my resident training in psychiatry I interviewed at Northwestern University where Dr. Jules Masserman, one of the foremost psychoanalysts of his day, was chief of the department. Dr. Masserman was an avowed Freudian who considered religion to be a neurosis and the belief in God as nothing but a remnant of the juvenile wish for a powerful, benevolent father.

You can imagine how he responded when I appeared for the interview in my traditional garb, including my beard. Dr. Masserman said early into our interview that my strong religious orientation might constitute an obstacle to my practicing pure "scientific" psychiatry. I replied that to the contrary I felt that belief in a higher power was an asset in recovery from both mental and physical disease and that this was true for both patient and therapist. I believed then and believe now that religion supports medicine.

As we were jousting, both of us maintaining our positions, we heard a loud thud. Outside the office the coatrack had been top-heavy and had fallen. Together we set the rack upright. Dr. Masserman noted that the rack was still leaning a bit and probably prone to fall again and suggested we turn it around so that it leaned against the wall. "That way if it falls, it will have something to fall back on."

"That's precisely the point I am making about religion," I said. Dr. Masserman smiled. Within a week I received a letter of acceptance to his residency program.

By following the Golden Rule we give each other a support system, a network, and the knowledge that even if one falls there is something to fall back on.

Chapter Three

ACTS OF KINDNESS
BOOST SELF-ESTEEM

Self love is the instrument of our preservation;
it resembles the provision for the perpetuity of mankind. . .

VOLTAIRE
"Self-Love," Philosophical Dictionary

Our sense of worth is tied to our self-esteem. To esteem something means to evaluate it. How do we evaluate our own worth to "esteem" ourselves? Think of the items you value either for their aesthetic or functional quality. A nonfunctioning grandfather clock is still valued because it is a beautiful piece of furniture. A nonfunctioning can opener is discarded because it is worthless. Not many of us can consider ourselves so handsome as to have enough aesthetic qualities to be our main purpose. Our value depends on our function. But just what is that function?

When one begins to purposefully perform acts of kindness, the spirit changes and soon doing good deeds becomes a focal point for our life; *doing* good begins to be the same as *feeling good*. The periods of emptiness when we search for the "meaning of it all" begin to fill with acts of kindness.

While a person's material contributions to society are important, productivity as a measure of worth is fallacious and dangerous. It isn't true that Mr. X is "worth" one million dollars. Mr. X has one million dollars. His worth is determined by his deeds. If we measure only productivity, how can we value the elderly who can no longer work? And what of those born with limitations? I have seen firsthand how overemphasizing conquests on the material plane is dangerous to self-esteem.

The Chinese have a curse, "May all your fondest dreams come true," which I did not understand until the son of a wealthy businessman came to me for counseling saying he was contemplating suicide.

This man's life was hardly a wreck. He owned a condo on the East Coast and a home on the West Coast, with a live-in lover in each. "I have a yacht and luxury cars, a stable of horses. There is nothing I want that I cannot obtain on a moment's notice." He was his father's only heir and had no reason nor drive to work. He avoided going to his office, because he was terrified that he might end up like his "crazy" workaholic father. What was paining my patient?

That's simple: he had no "reason" to feel good about himself. There was very little place in the world for his contributions and so he felt all his efforts at living were futile. I asked him the obvious question, "Haven't you thought about using your wealth to help others?" I counseled what anyone would have: that he could find much meaning in his life by donating time and money to help the needy, that he could gain self-satisfaction this way.

But the young man responded that his father had taught him to save money, not give it away. Good works were not an option.

I told this young man a story I remembered from my childhood about a man sentenced to years of hard labor. The man's hands were shackled to the handle of a huge, heavy wheel, mounted in the wall of his prison cell. During the countless days that he turned this heavy wheel, he would think about what his hard work was accomplishing. He imagined that the must be operating a mill that ground grain into flour, or perhaps a pump that brought water from a well to irrigate the land. At the end of his long imprisonment, when his shackles were removed, he promptly ran out to see what purpose the wheel served. But alas, it was attached to nothing! Just a huge wheel mounted in the wall! Bitter and tearful, the man collapsed. All those years of backbreaking work, all for nothing! If only there had been some purpose to his exertion, if only either man or animal had somehow benefited from his hard work, that would have redeemed his suffering. But to toil and labor for nothing! That was intolerable!

In the past century we have conquered frontiers that once were only in our dreams. But now sometimes it seems the magic of achievement has waned. So the question arises, how can we maintain our self-esteem?

The only territory left that offers us the thrill of exploration is found in doing for others, in reaching outside ourselves. This territory is wide open, with room enough for all of humanity. If this young man had not been programmed to horde his money and time, who knows what doors might have opened for him. As it is, though he did not literally commit suicide, I have learned he has developed a heroin habit and can no longer even enjoy his two homes, mistresses, horses, and other toys.

Oh, yes, there is still the territory of outer space to be conquered, and I am sure that the astronauts who return to Earth after walking on the Moon or rendezvousing with an orbiting satellite indeed feel a sense of accomplishment, as they should. But few of us can participate in these dramatic events. However, there is the conquest of an "outer space" that is accessible to everyone, the space outside of oneself. When we go beyond the confines of our "selfs" and extend ourselves to others, we are conquering "outer space," and, like the astronauts, we will have every reason to feel good.

The Stonecutter

There was a stonecutter who earned his livelihood by hewing rocks from the mountain. This was backbreaking as well as spirit-breaking work, and he would often curse his fate. "Why was I destined to be so lowly and humble? Why are other people so wealthy and mighty while I break my bones every day from dawn to dusk to put food on my table?"

One day, as he was engaged in this reverie, he heard a loud tumult in the distance. He climbed to the top of the mountain and could see a parade far off. The king was passing by, and on either side of the road there were throngs of people shouting, "Bravo," and throwing flowers at the royal coach.

"How wonderful it is to be great and powerful," the stonecutter thought. "I wish that I could be king."

As he spoke, he did not know that this happened to be his moment of grace, during which his wishes would be granted, and he suddenly found himself transformed. He was no longer a stonecutter. He was the king, clad in ermine, sitting in the royal coach drawn by white horses and receiving the acclaim of the crowd. "How wonderful it is to be the mightiest in all the land!"

After a while, however, he began to feel uncomfortable. The bright sun was shining down on him, making him sweat and squirm in his royal robes. "What is this?" he thought. "If I am the mightiest in the land then nothing should be able to affect me. If the sun can humble me, then the sun is mightier than I. But I wish to be the mightiest of all! I wish to be the sun."

Immediately he was transformed into the sun. He felt his mighty, unparalleled force. He could give light and warmth to everything in the world. It was his energy that made vegetation grow. He could provide warmth when he so wished or devastating fires when he was angry. "I am indeed the mightiest of all," he said to himself.

But suddenly he found himself very frustrated. He wished to direct his rays at a given point, but was unable to do so. A great cloud had moved beneath him and obstructed his rays. "Here, here!" he said. "If I am the mightiest, then nothing should be able to hinder me. If a cloud can frustrate the sun, then the cloud is mightier, yet I wish to be the mightiest. I wish to be a cloud!"

As a great, heavy cloud, he felt very powerful, dumping torrents of rain wherever he wished, and blocking the mighty sun. But his joy was short-lived, for suddenly he was swept away by a sharp gust of wind against which he felt himself helpless.

"Aha!" he cried. "The wind is even mightier than a cloud! Then I shall be the wind."

Transformed into the wind, he roared over oceans, churning immense waves. He blew over forests, toppling tall trees as if they were toothpicks. "Now I am truly the mightiest," he said.

But suddenly he felt himself stymied. He had come up against a tall mountain, and blow as he might, he could not get past. "So," he said, "a mountain is mightier than the wind! Then I wish to be a mountain."

As a tall mountain, he stood majestically, his peak reaching above the clouds. He was indeed formidable. Neither wind nor sun could affect him. Now he was indeed the mightiest.

All at once he felt a sharp pain. What was this? A stonecutter with a sharp pickax was tearing pieces out of him. "How can this be?" he asked. "If someone can dismember me then he must be even mightier than I. I wish to be that man." His wish was granted, and he was transformed into the mightiest of all: a stonecutter.

A while back a young man consulted me, seeking advice regarding a choice of medical specialties. He was a radiology resident, but was dissatisfied with that specialty. He was considering either psychiatry or anesthesiology. Prior to radiology he had served a year's residence in internal medicine, but did not like that specialty. Prior to medical school he had gone to engineering college, but had left there after one year. Now he wished to know what I recommended he do.

I told him a story. About a stonecutter.

The Golden Rule Can Mean
Give Yourself as You Are
to Your Neighbor

Early in my medical training I was assigned a patient in the hospital for one of the many horrendous effects of multiple sclerosis. This woman was young, maybe in her forties, and would have been in the prime of her life but her disease had rendered her bound to a wheelchair, in constant excruciating pain, unable to care for herself, never mind her children, and despondent. On the first day that I attended to her, I attempted to pull her out of the listless depression that hung like a cloud over her. When my efforts at feeble humor and chatty conversation failed I approached her directly, asking her if she needed to talk.

"What is there to say, doctor," she said in a voice quieted by emotional pain. "I don't have a reason to live. I can't take care of myself or my children. I'm stuck forever in this wheelchair. I can't perform the simplest task for myself. Why is God keeping me alive? Why, doctor?"

I had no answer, but I was terribly troubled by her circumstance and so I consulted my father, a much revered spiritual counselor. He cut right to the essence of this situation, saying, "You are only worried about your inability to solve her problem, not by the problem itself. This woman has a purpose if she can accept it and it is to live in the state she is in and offer to her family and other loved ones the wherewithal to care for her and comfort her and perform those deeds that will keep her life going. You can only help her accept. Not as glamorous perhaps as curing her, but probably more important."

He was right, my dear father. I had let my ego get in the way. Doctors in general feel helpless when we can't beat disease and I am no exception. The next day when I visited my patient I approached her with a different attitude. I did not think of her as a helpless and sorry victim. I saw her as a model to emulate and a testament to human courage. This didn't make a difference at first, but day after day I approached her in the same way until finally I could feel her spirit pick up as she absorbed my respect for her. From that day until she was discharged, my patient no longer wallowed in her bed, but sat propped up, with a bloom in her cheeks that was most likely a result of her taking time to make up. When she got back into her chair she moved around the hallways with energy, joked with the nursing staff. Most satisfying to me was the day I found her two sons visiting her and saw how loving and caring the trio was, with each of them caring for the other in turn.

A year later I received a Hanukkah card from her with a picture of the whole family, her in her wheelchair, smiling. She was surrounded by her loved ones. This truth is so simple it is sometimes hard to recognize: no step taken for another is futile. And because this truth is so simple it is imperative that we look at it with fresh eyes.

I have faith in man's inherent goodness. But sometimes we need to be reminded, to be encouraged to open our eyes and see all the opportunities that we have to be kind to others.

It is disastrous to feel that one isn't needed or wanted. And it's not only on the material plane that we hunger to find meaning. Most of us ask ourselves questions of purpose that go beyond the routines of our daily lives. We have at least fleeting thoughts about the broader reasons for our existence. It is a rare person who doesn't once in a while wonder why she is here. The obvious answer is to be kind to one another, to help another if he is in need, to perform good deeds.

As a doctor, I am aware that the medical staff in hospitals frequently take much longer to respond to a flash from a terminal patient than to calls from others. Whether the patient is conscious or not, this leaves a harmful impression on him if we write off his condition as being futile or pointless. Recently I looked in on a patient who was very ill, in fact close to death. He had been diagnosed with cancer during the time that we were working together. I took a peek at his chart and realized there was not a thing that could be done for him. But I did not want him to feel unnecessary, to feel that the short remainder of his earthly being was unimportant. And so I sat beside him, and stroked his hand. When I left him I knew that I had honored his being, and so neither one of was left feeling futile.

Our Purpose for Living
Is What We Are Doing
Right Now—Make It Good!

This is a story I learned in rabbinical school.

The great sage Eliezer fell gravely ill, and was visited by several of his students. Each student expressed copious gratitude for the master's teachings, telling him that he was more precious to them than the sun and the rain and even their own parents because all these had provided them only with earthly life, whereas the master had given them the key to eternal life. The Rabbi did not acknowledge any of this homage.

Then one student, Akiva, said, "Suffering, too, can be precious," to which Eliezer finally responded, saying, "Help me sit up so that I can hear what my child Akiva has to say."

The Rabbi had been despondent, because of the lack of self-esteem he suffered as a result of his disabling disease. To look back on the great achievements of the past was not much comfort when he was struggling with feelings of futility in the present. Admittedly he had been useful in the past, but what purpose did his life now serve?

Akiva's insight was powerful. His message was: a person is obligated to do only that which he is capable of doing. "There were times when you were able to teach and at those times that was your assignment. Now that your illness has taken that capability from you, it is no longer your duty. Perhaps your assignment now is to accept your suffering with equanimity, with trust and faith. You will set an example. At another stage in life your teaching was indeed precious. Even your present suffering can be precious, if you can accept it with serenity."

Self-esteem is essential. Gloria Steinem said in her autobiography, *Revolution from Within*, "I began to understand that self-esteem isn't everything; it's just that there's nothing without it." And by this I imagine her to mean that if she did not gain self-love there would have been no reason to begin a movement to help so many others. Where would we be if Gloria Steinem had not gained the self-esteem to go the distance? In working with patients who have been tyrannized by hedonistic desires, I have seen the incredible damage that can be caused by a tortured lack of self-esteem. Without a sense of worth, we might as well crumble and die.

The sage Hillel, whose teaching is the theme of this book, also said: "If I am not for myself, then who is for me? But if I am only for myself, just what am I?"

By this Hillel meant that a person must have a sense of self, i.e., knowing his strength and his abilities, but not be aware only of oneself which is egocentricity. If I am only for me then I am pointless. Bottom line: I should appreciate myself, but my goal should be to do for others.

Love Yourself as
Well as Your Neighbor

Rabbi Yisrael Meir Kagan, who is known among my people as the Chofetz Chaim (meaning one who truly loves life), was traveling home in his horse drawn carriage when he saw a man walking along the road. On inquiring he found that the man was headed to his own town and he offered the traveler a lift.

They began conversing and the man said that he was on his way to meet the greatest sage of the era, the Chofetz Chaim, for the first time. The Rabbi, who was the epitome of humility, did not tell the traveler who he was, rather he just shrugged his shoulders, "Why would you want to see him? He is just an ordinary person like everyone else."

The man became infuriated. "How dare you speak so disrespectfully about the greatest holy man of our time!" And the man accompanied his reprimand with a slap to Rabbi Kagan's face.

When they arrived at their destination the man was shocked to discover that the person he had slapped was none other than the great man himself and he apologized profusely.

Rabbi Kagan smiled, "There is no need to apologize," he said. "After all you were defending my honor. But this taught me something. I have been preaching how wrong it is to speak disparagingly about others. Now I know it is also wrong to speak disparagingly about oneself!"

The spiritual translation of "Do unto others as you would do unto yourself" is "love your neighbor as yourself," because by doing for others we are loving ourselves. When we love ourselves, we love our neighbor. We and our neighbor essentially become a single self.

Chapter Four

GOOD DEEDS
CREATE LOVE

Love is, above all, the gift of oneself.

JEAN ANOUILH
Ardele

Mitzvah *Is* Unconditional Love

One of the most simple yet profound ideas concerning love's relationship to the Golden Rule was expressed by my forefather, the Baal Shem Tov, who said that the road to loving God is the love of mankind. Or to state his meaning another way: we cannot reach God directly, but only through loving other people. So while "doing the right thing" is the basic principle to explain *how* we do unto others, creating love is the reason *why*.

Creating love is a lesson which cannot be taught, but only experienced. Long ago I learned this from one of my patients.

For eighteen years Edith was married to an alcoholic. She had spent many years adjusting to her husband, Fred's, addiction. Nevertheless, Edith longed to raise a family, but after several years of marriage it was apparent that she was not likely to conceive. When she consulted a specialist, this in the days before high-tech fertility was popular, he told her she must make peace with the fact that she would never have children. This was about the time Edith came into therapy. After coping with her anger and resentment, Edith and her husband adopted two children, and about this same time the husband gave up his drinking.

The family settled down, and managed to lead a fairly happy and healthy life for several years. Then, one winter, Edith felt ill. She was forty-two years old at the time, and thinking that she had the flu, she went to a doctor. You know the end of this part of the story: she was pregnant! The miracle they had prayed for had happened. Her child would be a Rhodes Scholar! She was sure of it.

But the reality was far different, far more difficult. The little boy was born with Down's syndrome. Edith speaks for herself: "I thought I had divested myself of all anger, bitterness and resentments, but they all returned in a crescendo when I held Timmy in my arms for the first time. I questioned God. Why had He done this to me? Why had He so cruelly teased me?

"Every night Fred and I stood over Timmy's crib and prayed to God. 'God, we know you can do it. You have done so many miracles. Just this one time, grant us our wish. Change him, God, change him.' We thought if only God would change our baby, somehow all life's problems would be solved.

"We prayed incessantly for a miracle, and then one day it happened. God changed *us*, and we accepted Timmy with all the love in the world, accepting him just as he was.

"Now I know it was all worth it. I sit in the rocker, holding Timmy in my arms. I look at his funny little eyes and at his pudgy hands where there is only one crease instead of the usual two, and I think how much I love my child in spite of his defects. Then I know, I know for certain, that God loves me, in spite of all *my* defects."

The Woman in the Hat

The Jewish mystics believe that when God loves someone He provides them an opportunity to do a good deed. The following happened shortly before my dear wife died and I am forever thankful that God gave me this opportunity to ease her mind.

There is a woman who spends much time near the Western Wall in Jerusalem, collecting money for the poor. Because she always wears a hat to shield herself from the tropical sun my wife and I referred to her as the "Hat Lady." The Hat Lady is well known to be authentic and reliable about seeing that the money gets to the needy. During Goldie's illness, when we were in Israel I made one of my visits to the Western Wall to pray. As I was leaving, my wife said, "If you see the Hat Lady, give her some money."

Needless to say my prayers were fervent. My wife's doctor had told me that there was no "light at the end of the tunnel," and while I hoped for a miracle I was preparing myself to accept what would be with serenity. However, I wished to be in God's good graces to see me through what lay ahead, which is why I prayed so fervently. Yet when I looked around I could not find the Hat Lady. From this I drew the conclusion that God did not love me enough to give me the opportunity to perform a good deed. That hurt.

Just as I was about to board the bus leaving the Old City, I noticed her, the lady with the hat, arriving. I can't remember when I've felt a thrill like that. This was God's message to me: "I may be dealing you a heavy blow, but I still love you."

You Can Only Give
What You Have

I think often of Scott, a gentleman who came from Chicago to Gateway for treatment. He was arrogant, a trait which his wife assured us had been a part of him way before his addiction spun out of control. He was also verbally abusive and abrasive: most noticeably he was cold, as unreachable as the bottom of an iceberg.

On the day he was to return home I was out of the center and missed his departure. I knew what time his flight was leaving and since my journey that day took me past the airport, I stopped and somehow talked my way past the desk agent and onto the plane (being dressed in traditional Chassidic garb has its advantages). Scott was surprised, of course, to see me walking down the aisle toward him and when he stood, I hugged and kissed him as I said good-bye. Scott's eyes welled up with tears. "That's the first time anyone other than Susan (his wife) has been so kind and loving to me."

Two weeks later Scott returned for a brief stay in the Center. During his first stay his icy demeanor had been addressed but he always dismissed it. Now he was able to face the truth about himself: he grasped suddenly that he could not give what he had never received. This must have been an epiphany because Scott was like a different, much warmer person from then on in the groups and informal exchanges.

Eight years later I was changing planes at O'Hare when I ran into Scott and Susan. We caught each other up. They were on their way to a skiing trip in the Alps to celebrate their twenty-fifth anniversary. His wife said, "Without Gateway there never would have been a twenty-fifth anniversary."

Like the story I once told Avi about the diamond, Scott had given his wife a perfect gem for her anniversary; the very finest polished diamond which was himself and all the love he had to give.

And all of this just because I had said good-bye to a person of whom I'd grown fond.

You Can't Keep It
Unless You Give It Away

John's marriage was going nowhere. He consulted the Yellow Pages and met with an attorney who specialized in divorce. After hearing John's troubles the lawyer agreed to take the case. John was surprised that the lawyer's fee was only $500, which was to be paid in one month's time when the documents had been prepared for John's signature.

"But," the attorney said, "you must follow my instructions exactly as I give them. On the way home, buy your wife a little gift and do this every week until you see me again. Every day you must find something nice to say to her whether you feel that way or not and under no circumstances are you to raise your voice. In this way perhaps you will ameliorate the pain she'll suffer over the divorce."

A month later John was at the lawyer's office. "I'm not sure that I want to proceed with the divorce," he said. "We seem to be getting along much better."

The lawyer nodded. "Very well then. And I'm not surprised. It happens quite often that people change their mind."

"How much money do I owe you for drawing up the documents?"

The lawyer smiled. "There are no documents. I was pretty sure you wouldn't be needing them."

Some months later John was in the neighborhood where the lawyer kept his office. It looked a bit different but he stopped in anyway, wanting to thank the attorney for being such a lifesaver.

"Is Alan in?" he asked the woman at the reception desk, which had not been there before. "Has he moved offices?"

"There's no Alan, here, sir. We've been running our insurance company here for fifteen years. Are you sure you're in the right place?"

John double-checked, remembering landmarks and the exact address. For a few days this bothered him. He thought he might be losing his mind. But soon he accepted that Alan was whatever or whomever he was and he came to John at the right time.

And that's one way God loves us; He gives us what we need, or who, when we need it so we can give it back again to someone else.

The Good Son's Good Deed

The Talmud tells the story of Dama ben Netina, a merchant who had a precious stone that was needed for the breastplate of the high priest. He had been offered an enormous sum for the stone. However, the key to his strongbox was under the pillow upon which his father was sleeping and rather than risking awakening his father, he let the deal go.

A year later Dama ben Netina was rewarded for his loving *mitzvah*. A pure red heifer was born in his herd. The red heifer is very rare and used for one of the most sacred rituals in the temple. Because it is so rare, it is priceless.

Dama ben Netina, who performed this *mitzvah* with no expectation of compensation, was thus rewarded for having given his father devotion and respect.

Sometimes a good deed is taking care of the people you love.

Chapter Five

DOING FOR OTHERS CREATES HAPPINESS— FOR THEM, FOR YOU

That action is best which procures the greatest happiness for the greatest numbers.

HOMER
Odyssey

If there is one universal truth, it is that each one of us seeks happiness. Yet we cannot truly pursue happiness if we don't know what it is.

The darling of Chassidic lore, Rabbi Levi Yitzchok, once saw a man hurrying frenetically through the marketplace. "My dear fellow," he said, stopping the man, "please pause for a moment and tell me where are you running to?"

"I'm sorry, sir," the man said, "but I can't stop now. I am in pursuit of my happiness."

Rabbi Levi Yitzchok said: "But how do you know that your happiness lies in the direction you are heading? Perhaps it is the other way and you are really running from it?"

Rabbi Levi Yitzchok's question points to a simple truth which we have all experienced, whether consciously or not: the search for happiness in things outside ourselves will never work. To want happiness for another is centrifugal, and like the rays that extend outward from the sun, bringing light to all, the happiness spreads everywhere, both over oneself as well as others. To envy others or wish them ill is centripetal, turning in on oneself, and like the black hole of astronomy, swallowing the light so that one is left in the darkness of misery. Just as light and darkness cannot coexist, neither can benevolence and malevolence. The easiest way to accrue happiness for oneself is to wish it for another.

Reflections

Rabbi Meir of Premislan once heard the complaint of a congregant who worried that another retailer had opened a store in competition with him. "Did you ever watch a horse drink from a stream?" the Rabbi asked. "You will notice that he taps with his hoof while drinking.

"The horse sees his reflection in the water and thinks that there is another horse there who will drink all the water and that there will be none left for him. He therefore taps with his hoof in an attempt to scare the other horse away.

"Do not be like the horse. There is enough in the world for both you and your competitor. He will not take away what is destined for you."

After this the storekeeper gave help, tips and advice to the other retailer and both of them prospered, each store, as is often the case, fueling the other.

Happiness Is Relative

Remember the adage, "I cried because I had no shoes until I saw a man who had no feet"? Does the man with no feet gain a *mitzvah* from just his poor fortune? Or from appearing when he does? I think the latter, and Nora's story, below, explains why.

Nora was eight months sober when she came to me for a consultation. I was in a terrible mood that day. My brand-new car, which had cost me tons of money, had a defect: the cruise control was not accurate. This meant I would have to take it back to the dealer for an adjustment. I didn't have that kind of time.

Nora told me how fortunate she was. She was beginning to reap some of the rewards of sobriety. She had found an apartment she could afford for herself and her son, and a steady job albeit at minimal wage. She was happy, for the first time in so long, maybe even forever. In fact she hoped she might be able to save enough money to get her car fixed.

"What's wrong with your car?" I asked.

"There's no reverse. The reverse gear is broken."

"How do you drive without reverse?"

"Oh, you have to plan things out, like how to park so you don't have to back up. But I must remember, some people don't even have a car."

I am positive that Nora's coming in for an unscheduled appointment was God's way of reprimanding me for being ungrateful for my new car, with power steering, brakes, windows, air conditioner—and reverse—and for being so petty about the cruise control.

Incidentally, Nora spreads happiness another way: she visits cancer patients and shows them her long hair together with a picture of her bald head when she was on chemo. "My hair is thicker than ever," she says. "It used to be hard to manage. Chemo was the greatest thing to happen to my hair."

This wonderful lady provides a magic ingredient to the people she consoles, one that can aid their therapy.

Good Deeds Are Contagious

Elijah the Prophet told a sage that two people, whom the prophet identified, were assured of a place in heaven. The sage then asked the two men what they did to warrant this reward. They said that they stayed in the marketplace, and when they saw someone with a sad face, they would try and cheer them up. What an easy way to get to heaven.

This reminds me of a more modern tale: a young woman I know is battling cancer. Frequently, when she is feeling strong physically but a little down, she purchases a bunch of carnations or daisies and goes to the large mall near her home where she proceeds to hand out flowers, each accompanied by a smile. This idea came to her in a cancer support group where the importance of cheerfulness and good attitude are never undervalued. As most of us know by now, there is little doubt that there is a corollary between mental attitude and wellness. The giving of the flowers with a smile makes the recipient momentarily gay; she smiles in return and this small touch of joy can literally change her brain and affect her fight against cancer. Making good things happen for others creates happiness, for them, for you.

Mississippi's Angel

Is there anyone who has not heard the story of Oseola McCarty of Hattiesburg, Mississippi? Her good deed created happiness for others and, though she didn't expect it, for herself as well.

In 1995 Ms. McCarty made a contribution of $150,000 to the University of Southern Mississippi to finance scholarships. This would not be exceptional, except that she had made this money as a washerwoman, saving every penny she'd earned from lifting, scrubbing, washing, tending, to give away to student strangers she might never know. At the time of the gift she was eighty-eight. She never married and had taken care of all the women in her family and as they died off one by one leaving her alone, she struggled on.

She never would have dreamed the happiness this *mitzvah* would bring back to her. In the year after her gift Roberta Flack sang her a song; Patti Labelle did as well. President Clinton honored her. Harvard gave her an honorary degree.

Whoopi Goldberg knelt at her feet to talk with her. Oseola, everyone says, gives off a feeling of peace and that is part of the reason people come to see her.

But sometimes she's been flown to them. Before flying to New York, Ms. McCarty had never been out of Mississippi before. She had no idea she could eat on an airplane. She was flown all around the country to accept humanitarian awards. All the hotel maids adored her because she made her own bed. She even got a book contract. And, perhaps best of all, according to the woman whom the university appointed to assist her, Jewel Tucker, "It has been like watching a flower open. Nothing of value was lost in her transformation. I see her at dinners in her French silk shoes and then I see her at night when she gets down on her knees to pray."

How many students will be able to go to college because of Ms. McCarty we cannot say. But even before one dollar has been spent, look at how many people's lives have been touched, most especially hers.

A Mixed Bag

I have been fortunate to know many spiritual people. These people have invariably dedicated themselves to some form of work outside of themselves, and never to the pursuit of self-gratification for its own sake. Performing good gave meaning to their lives. When necessary, goodness enabled them to survive great adversity, and also to feel a measure of joy in times of great sadness. They understood, too, that to perform good deeds is to accomplish God's assignment for us. Only the person who lives a life which transcends his own being can rejoice even while he is dealing with his own suffering. Rabbi Chaim-Cheskel Wrona was just such a man.

Chaim-Cheskel was an itinerant rabbi who had come to America shortly before World War II hoping to bring his family after him, but this wish was thwarted by the outbreak of war. Alone in America, Wrona would frequently visit my boyhood home in Milwaukee during his travels, and on one of his visits my father prevailed upon him to settle in the city, since I was in need of a religious instructor. The Rabbi agreed, and soon acquired a number of students.

Of course, during the war there was no way of getting any news about the whereabouts of the Wrona family in Poland. After the war, news of the Holocaust began to trickle from Europe to the United States, and the Rabbi learned that he had lost his wife and children in the death camps. He grieved at the same time that he continued to teach the children of his adopted community.

One day the Rabbi received a letter from a Holocaust survivor who had somehow traced him to Milwaukee. This person confirmed what he already knew, that his wife and children had been among the millions to perish at the hands of the Nazis.

But the writer also had another story to tell. He relayed that Chaim-Cheskel's son had been assigned to work in the crematorium in Auschwitz, and had managed to smuggle some explosives into the camp. In the hope of slowing down the killings and possibly saving some lives, he had blown himself up along with some of the crematorium equipment. Upon learning this news, Rabbi Chaim-Cheskel Wrona wept profusely, yet even as this news reopened his wound he expressed great gratitude to the writer of the letter for having given him a gift: the story of his son's magnificent deed.

A mere three weeks later, during the holiday *Simchas Torah,* in which Jews celebrate their holy book, Chaim-Cheskel danced in jubilation. As a young man at the time, I was bewildered by the Rabbi's mixed display of emotions. I wondered how he could be bowed down with grief and so shortly thereafter literally dancing with unbounded joy.

Many years later, however, I finally understood the Rabbi's acceptance of both joy and grief, sometimes mixed up together. I understood because a kindness done for me by others made me feel joy and sadness in the same moment.

Goldie, my wife of forty years, had passed away, and the memory of losing her is still unbearable for me to think about. Early in our marriage we had introduced a man and a woman to each other. This couple had married and had six children, and those children had always considered us ersatz grandparents. They were always in and out of our house. About the same time as Goldie had died, one of these children had married and become pregnant. When this baby was born, the young couple called me with a message that was truly a *mitzvah:* they wanted to name the baby girl Goldie. At that moment, I thought of Chaim-Cheskel, who had danced and wept at the same time. It hurt to be reminded of my Goldie's passing yet it was joyful to realize she would in some way live on through this baby girl.

In my darkest hours, I have found that others' acts of kindness remove me from the shadows. And when someone else is in pain I know now a little better how to pull them through.

As I matured I realized how special was Chaim-Cheskel's capacity to feel joy for us, his adopted community, and for the people his son saved from the ovens, even though wracked with pain and grief over his personal tragedy. His ability to take part in our celebration was one of his *mitzvahs*. His ability to feel joy for those his son saved is the very essence of *mitzvah.* Chaim-Cheskel taught me much about the Golden Rule.

Izik's Folly

In Kraców there stands a synagogue known as the Shul of Izik Reb Yekale's. Legend has it that Izik was a simple man, a builder by trade, who was haunted by the same dream over and over again, that under a particular bridge in Prague was buried a huge treasure, which would belong to whomever unearthed it.

At first Izik dismissed this dream as absurd, but after a while he became obsessed, and could hardly sleep at night. Although his wife told him to get the crazy idea out of his head, he decided once and for all that he must go to Prague and find the treasure. So, one day he took some meager provisions and set out for Prague.

When Izik was fortunate enough to hitch a ride on a passing wagon, he rode. Otherwise he walked, stopping only at nightfall, sleeping in the shelter of the trees.

After many weeks, Izik arrived at Prague and sought out the bridge he had envisioned in his dream. But alas, the police were always patrolling the area and there was no way he could begin to dig.

For days he loitered near the bridge, hoping that perhaps there would be a break in the patrol, allowing him time to dig for the treasure. Finally one of the police patrols approached him. "Why are you constantly loitering around this area day after day?" the policeman asked. "What is it you want here?"

Izik was a simple man, and saw no other way but to tell the truth. He related his dream to the policeman, also telling him of the travail of the long journey he had made in order to get to Prague from his humble village near Kraców.

When Izik had finished telling his story, the policeman howled with laughter. "You fool!" he said. "And because of a silly dream you came all the way here? Well, I have had a repetitious dream, too. I have been dreaming that in a tiny village near Kraców there is a little hut that belongs to an idiot named Izik Reb Yekale's, and that in that hut there is a tremendous treasure. Believe me, friend, there is no treasure for you here."

Crushed, Izik returned home, only to find that in his absence the plans he had set in motion before chasing a dream were actually coming to fruition: his hopes to build a bigger house were finally realized because the price of lumber had fallen drastically; the lot he had his heart set on was available and affordable since the owners had left the area and the rumor was that they had instructed their agent to unload the land quickly, at any price. Best of all, his wife had discovered that they were to have a child. Out of all this good fortune Izik Reb Yekale's prospects flourished, and he was able to build not only a bigger house for his growing family, but a large new synagogue for his community. He considered building the temple was his *mitzvah* in return for having learned a valuable lesson.

Neither wealth, fame, prestige, nor anything external can give us more than a fleeting sense of satisfaction. As corny as it sounds, the only true lasting happiness is within ourselves—which, sadly, is too often the last place any of us look for it.

Gems of Life

In 1311, King Philip of France decreed the expulsion of all Jews from the land, ordering them to be gone within two days under penalty of death. Obviously there was no time to sell their belongings.

One of the exiles was a wealthy dealer in gems and knew that his precious stones would be confiscated as he left the country. He therefore secreted a bag of jewels with his neighbor, thinking that one day the decree might be revoked. Sure enough when King Philip died many years later, his son inherited the throne and revoked the decree. Some of the exiles returned, the jeweler among them. The first thing he did was to try and find his neighbor to whom he had entrusted his treasure, but the man was nowhere to be found.

Upon inquiring, he learned that his neighbor had become destitute, had sold all his belongings including his fine home and had fallen into a deep depression. He now lived as a hermit in a small hut outside the city. Obviously if the man had sold everything the jewels would be gone.

Nevertheless he made his way to the outskirts of the city and found his neighbor in a sorry state, lean with hunger and shivering from the cold. When he entered the hut, the neighbor said, "At last you have come! Now I can die." He then reached into a box and drew forth the bag with the jewels.

"When my fortune went against me, I tried desperately to save myself by borrowing money and doing business, but rather than profit I lost everything. All my belongings that I sold could not cover my debts, and I had to leave the city in disgrace. Many times I felt that my life was not worth living and I thought of taking my life to escape this misery. But how could I do that? You had entrusted your jewels to me and if I died, you would have no way of retrieving them if you ever returned. I therefore had to remain alive to return your diamonds to you. Now that I have done so, I can die in peace."

The jeweler tearfully embraced his neighbor. "You shall not die now. These jewels are worth a fortune. We shall buy a home together and live as devoted friends forever."

Good deeds have the magic to turn sadness to singing and despair to joy. Try it. Just one small selfless act, when you are feeling blue, can turn your day around. Goodness creates a bouquet of profound feelings in both the giver and receiver. Joy, for certain; love and connectedness, self-esteem. All these feelings have the power to change the way we conduct ourselves in this world.

Chapter Six

KINDNESS TOWARD STRANGERS

Man, by definition, is born a stranger: coming from nowhere, he is thrust into an alien world which existed before him——a world which didn't need him. And which will survive him.

ELIE WIESEL
The Kingdom of Memory

Boruchovich's Good Deed

To respond to Mr. Wiesel's quote on the previous page: because what he says is so true, if we can't rely on the kindness of strangers we're in big trouble.

In Berdichev there lived a man who was struggling to eke out a meager living to support his family. This man had grandiose aspirations and repeatedly told his wife he wanted to go to Leipzig, a nearby city, to seek his fortune, but his wife resisted.

"What will become of me and the children then?" she would wail. "It's bad enough we are starving, but if you leave, we will also be abandoned. How would you expect me to support these two children if you were gone?"

One day the man came home with good news. "I have been hired by Boruchovich to represent his interests in Leipzig. He will pay me well. Every Friday you are to report to his office to receive my salary. I must leave immediately since he is negotiating several major deals right now."

The wife, assured of more than an adequate income, helped her husband pack his things and soon he was on his way to the city.

On that Friday, she reported to Boruchovich's office as instructed and gave the cashier her husband's name. The cashier was perplexed. "We don't have an employee by that name," he said.

The woman told the cashier that her husband had been hired by Boruchovich just that week to represent his interests in Leipzig. The cashier checked his records again, and then told the woman that she was mistaken, because they had no record of anyone by that name being added to the payroll.

The woman suddenly realized that her husband had deceived her. Her worst fears had come true. She was now alone and destitute. She began to weep bitterly.

Boruchovich, who was working in his office, heard the crying and came out to investigate. The cashier explained how the woman had been duped by her husband.

"Oh, for heaven's sake," said Boruchovich. "It had totally slipped my mind to inform you," he said to the cashier. Then he turned to the woman and said, "Your husband told you the truth. My agent in Leipzig died and I hired your husband, but so many things happened this week I forgot to tell the cashier. Yes, you are to come every Friday for his pay."

More than a year passed during which the husband in Leipzig was successful in business and returned, finally, to Berdichev with adequate funds to establish himself in business. He expected to find his family destitute, his wife and children hungry and in rags. He also expected to be greeted with a shower of curses from his wife but he hoped she would ultimately forgive him for his deception now that he could provide amply for the family.

How astonished he was when his wife and children, well-dressed and in good health, embraced him. After a bit he cautiously got the story from his wife and learned that Boruchovich had covered for him. A few days later he calculated all he owed to Boruchovich and went to pay his debt, but the man refused him. "I was happy to support your family. I will not sell the happiness this brought me for money."

Boruchovich was a notorious cheapskate, believe it or not, but this story, as well as the one earlier in the book and a few others in my family's mythology, show how he changed his character over the course of his life through acts of kindness!

The Life You Save
May Be Your Own

Marc Anthony said, "The good [men do] is oft interred with their bones."

I disagree.

While I was going for my degree in psychiatry I learned of one psychiatrist, Phillipe Pinel, who revolutionized care for the mentally ill. In 1793, conditions for patients were deplorable. At that time, Dr. Pinel removed the shackles of mental patients in a French asylum. "Are you insane yourself," his colleagues asked, "that you unchain these beasts?"

During the French Revolution Pinel was falsely accused of harboring enemies of the people, and a mob tried to lynch him. He was saved by a huge muscular man who fought off the mob. This man was one of those whose shackles Pinel had removed.

You Never Have to Be Alone

There was a group of observant Jews who always met before dawn to begin morning prayers. The one member of the community who never appeared was a living legend named Rabbi Moshe-Leib. The Rabbi explained that he couldn't appear at this time because that was when he ascended to Heaven.

Well, you can imagine the gossip and barbs about this: "He's too lazy for a Rabbi," one shul member would say and then, "I think I'll ascend at dawn tomorrow too—do you think I'll run into the Rabbi?" The men all laughed. But one member of Rabbi Moshe-Leib's congregation, Yonah, did not find this funny. It bothered him that his spiritual leader was not able to show up for morning service, arguably the most necessary and important service of the day. So Yonah developed a plan.

On a Wednesday in October Yonah hid behind a large chinaberry tree whose long weeping limbs hid him completely. Before the early rays of the sun appeared on the horizon, Rabbi Moshe-Leib emerged from his home, not with a talis or tefillin, but rather clothes that gave the suggestion he was about to work outdoors. Yonah followed the Rabbi at a safe distance and with steps so quiet his wife would never have believed it was really him. Once the Rabbi looked over his shoulder and Yonah ran to the side of the unpaved road and laid down as flat as he could get amidst the rough weeds and grass.

Just as the sun was up and it was officially dawn Yonah saw Rabbi Moshe-Leib knock on the door and then enter a tiny wooden cabin in the middle of nowhere, surrounded by woods. Yonah snuck to the one window, open to the breeze. There he saw an old woman sitting on a chair, wrapped in shawls. Yonah couldn't hear what they were saying but shortly Rabbi Moshe-Leib came out of the cabin with an ax and cut wood.

So this was it. How could the congregation have doubted him? How could he have doubted the Rabbi? As Yonah watched, the Rabbi reentered the cabin, to build and light the fire. From a small bag Yonah had not noticed, the Rabbi removed some food and gave it to the old woman. They talked for another few moments and then the Rabbi exited. Yonah, who was younger by far than most of the congregation, sprinted to the temple, putting distance between himself and the Rabbi so quickly that he wasn't seen.

When he arrived, a bit late for morning prayers, the congregation was still waiting because they needed ten men

to start and Yonah was the tenth. But before he would pre-
pare himself for prayer Yonah stood before his people and
said, "I have seen the Rabbi ascend, but it is not to Heaven."
There was grumbling but Yonah quickly silenced the group:
"He ascends much higher."

The Good Deed Dowry

Abraham, the biblical patriarch, welcomed weary wayfarers, providing them with food and drink. When he sent his trusted servant, Eliezer, to find a wife for his son, Isaac, the servant set up the following criteria:

"I will ask the maidens for a drink of water. The one who will fetch water for me and also offer to water my camels, that will be the appropriate person to enter my master's household."

Shortly afterward, the young shepherdess Rebecca appeared, and offered to fetch water not only for Eliezer, but for his camels as well. When the camels finished drinking, Rebecca said, "Perhaps you need a place to lodge. My father's home is spacious."

Eliezer knelt and thanked God. For his beloved master's home, Eliezer wanted only the woman with a golden heart. The trait of doing good for those she did not know even without their requesting it was the most important attribute he sought in a wife for the son of his holy master.

The Talmud relates that a miracle occurred in Isaac and Rebecca's home, in that the bread she baked was always enough for however many wayfarers paused to refresh themselves. This is a miracle we can easily duplicate in our own lives. Somehow, when we share with others, there always seems to be enough for all.

The Smallest Act of Kindness
Can Be Large

Whenever we reach outside ourselves and place the needs of others before our own, we rise, or ascend, above uncomfortable and self-defeating traits. I learned this lesson long ago, while I was still an intern. I was on duty at the hospital on Sundays. In those days there were no intravenous teams, so that only one person was authorized to administer intravenous medication, and that person was the intern on duty—and on Sundays that was me.

One day I was required to give intravenous medication to a patient whose private nurse told me that he was very depressed. The man had come into the hospital for surgery on his hip, but during the operation he had gone into cardiac arrest. His surgeon had quickly turned the patient on his back, opened his chest, and began pumping his heart manually. When the patient later awoke and found the bandages on his chest, he was shocked and scared.

Some instinct led me to suggest to the patient that we pray together. He was Catholic, he said, so I suggested the Twenty-third Psalm. When I said, "Though we walk through the valley of the shadow of death Thou art with me," the patient began crying. Overwhelmed myself by the power of his feeling, I wept along with him. After we finished the Psalm he squeezed my hand and said, "Thanks, Doc."

The following day I dropped by to see him, and the nurse told me that there had been a miraculous change in his attitude. He was sitting up in bed joking. He had a good appetite. As I entered the room he greeted me with a smile, and then explained:

"When I woke up from the operation and found out that my heart had stopped, I was shocked. It occurred to me that if it stopped once it could stop again anytime, but this time there might not be any doctor around to get it started. I was afraid I might die at any moment.

"But when together we said 'Though I walk through the valley of the shadow of death I will fear no evil for Thou art with me,' I realized that I was someone who had really been in the valley of the shadow of death. Hell, for those few moments when my heart wasn't beating I was dead!

"Then I began thinking: for thirty-five years I was a police officer, the last fifteen of them as a sergeant. I believe I helped many people, and in so doing I have tried to please God. I have every right to expect that when I die, He will be with me. That thought took the fear out of dying. Who knows how much time I have left, whether ten years or ten days? But whenever my time comes, I am no longer afraid. The antibiotics worked. But the prayer worked better."

Our praying together helped me as much as it helped him. I recognized that this small deed I offered a stranger drove away the anxiety and fear that his ruminating was causing him; it helped me to feel there was something I could do for him and seeing that it helped give me confidence. I learned that even the seemingly smallest acts of kindness could do so much for another person.

The Kindness of Strangers

After a struggle with heart disease, including several open-heart surgeries, Barney died at age thirty-seven. He had been unable to work for several years and his heart disease had precluded his getting life insurance. Barney's widow and two children were left without support.

Barney's parents had a family plot in a cemetery one thousand miles from Barney's home. His brother, Charles, flew ahead of the widow to accompany the body and became involved in a conversation with the passenger seated next to him, to whom he related the tragic events.

"You must establish an educational trust fund for the children," the man said. "Try to contact his friends and all your relatives and invest the money safely so that when the children reach college age the money will be there." The brother thanked the stranger for his advice.

Just as they alighted from the plane the man handed Charles an envelope. He later opened it to find five one-hundred-dollar bills and a note which read, "Let this be the first installment on the children's trust fund."

Five hundred dollars from a total stranger. Why, some might wonder. "A miracle!" some will say. "An angel, descended from heaven in the form of a human." No, not at all. Just a good deed, a *mitzvah* from one stranger to another. And just in case you think this is an isolated incident, Bruce Springsteen, New Jersey's own homegrown bona fide superstar, once gave $100,000 to an Arizona waitress he hardly knew because she couldn't afford seriously needed medical care.

Good Deeds Go
Wherever the Wind Blows

As kids we would blow the fluff from dandelions and watch the seeds hover in the air carried by the wind to wherever they would take root. Good deeds may be less tangible than dandelion seeds, but they too are blown by the wind without our knowing where they might take root and grow.

At the University of Pittsburgh's Western Psychiatric Institute, where I did my residency, there was a Korean doctor who told me he had been orphaned in the war. He had been cared for by an agency that received funds from charitable donors, mostly from the States. "I was able to eat and have clothes because someone gave money for hungry kids they did not know. Whenever I take care of a patient now I always think, 'This may be the person who saved my life.' And I am extra careful."

Mitzvahs *and Miracles*

The following story seems almost quaint, given the crosscurrents of faith and race that define our country in this time. But the very innocence of this *mitzvah* story pulls me to it; also as it happens the Jewish doctor was the father of a dear friend of mine.

An encounter occurred involving three religions, two races and one little boy battling polio. The child, who was known as Butch, was admitted by his family physician to a hospital in St. Louis, miles away from his home. He was stricken with polio and only the big-city hospitals would admit him.

Butch's father, Corwin S. Ruge, was a prominent banker in the small Wright City. He and his wife followed the ambulance that carried their son to St. Louis. By the second day of Butch's stay he was in a coma. The parents wept; there didn't seem too much else to do.

The boy's doctor was a senior resident, a Jew. When the Ruges asked if Butch had a chance the doctor said, "Only a miracle can save him." Whether or not the doctor meant the Ruges to take this literally or not doesn't matter. It was so accepted and the parents set out to find spiritual help.

They were Protestant and knew no ministers in St. Louis, but a young Catholic priest who frequently visited Wright City had a brother in St. Louis. Mr. Ruge contacted the brother who was able to put them in touch with a Catholic priest. The Ruges hurried out to the university where the priest resided. "Will you say a prayer for our little boy who is desperately ill?" asked Mr. Ruge. He would and did. Kneeling with the Ruges, the priest asked divine intercession that "this little Protestant boy's life might be spared."

Next morning the priest said a Mass at church. Several Catholic organizations took up the spiritual battle for the "little Protestant boy," and asked their members to pray for his recovery. Finally a radio station broadcast appealed for prayer.

When the parents returned to the hospital they learned that the Jewish physician had said a prayer for Butch and the African-American nurse had prayed without ceasing.

Two days passed and the boy had not improved. His life was ebbing fast. Mr. and Mrs. Ruge waited for the inevitable. Early the next morning the phone in their motel room rang and the doctor was on the line. "When I entered the ward this morning," he began, "Butch recognized me and smiled. His fever is gone."

Mr. Ruge exclaimed, "Doctor this is a miracle. My son has been raised from the dead by prayer."

Strangers' prayers, in fact. And I don't believe for a moment that this factor is of no consequence.

Little Things Mean a Lot

God considers small favors to strangers as good deeds. I learned this first from a gentleman who worked in my father's synagogue.

As a child I used to watch Mr. Fairman, the maintenance man, repair things. I was fascinated by his tools and he let me use them. One time I drove a nail into a piece of lumber (I loved to hammer nails!).

Mr. Fairman came to me, holding the board. "Do you know that some person might try to saw that piece of wood and ruin his equipment?" He then laboriously extracted the nail.

I was eight years old when this occurred. Sometimes I have forgotten to be considerate of a stranger, but whenever I realize I am in the process of being discourteous, I remember Mr. Fairman.

A small story in the Talmud about a meaningful consideration occurs to me: once a man was cleaning his garden and throwing rocks from it into the street. A man passing by stopped to say, "Why do you throw rocks from a property that is not yours into your own?" The man with the garden laughed at this absurd remark.

Before too long this man's business failed and he lost his home. Walking down the street, he stumbled on one of the rocks that he had thrown from his garden. As he rose to his feet he thought, "How right that wise man was! What I thought was mine was really not and it is the public street that is really my own."

Some may take this story literally, and think of the slogans about not littering. Sure, the sidewalk is yours, and you don't want to dirty it. But the message is really far-reaching.

Emotions can affect and distort our judgment. Our acquisitive drives may render us incapable of seeing that when we are inconsiderate of others in the pursuit of our own gain, we may profit in the short term, but so often our greed returns to haunt us. There are indeed many obstacles along the various paths in life, but some are those that we thoughtlessly put there ourselves. We may later stub our toes on the rocks that we threw out to improve our own property.

The Nun's Story

Shortly after I became Director of Psychiatry at St. Francis Hospital I received a call from Pittsburgh's Bishop (later Cardinal) Wright. He told me that as a result of the changes which occurred through Vatican II there was much turmoil in the convents. Some of the nuns were emotionally troubled but he was not comfortable consulting secular psychiatrists who might attribute their difficulties to the restrictions imposed by their vows. However, since I also was of a religious order he would feel at ease if I would oversee their treatment.

"Bishop," I complained, "I am already working a twenty-six-hour day at the hospital. I really cannot take on any additional responsibilities."

The Bishop pushed me a little. "Rabbi," he said, "you'll have a *mitzvah*." Obviously I couldn't refuse.

One of the things I discovered was that when a nun left the convent she was referred to as a "fugitive." I objected to this. A woman who had given so many years of her life to the church did not deserve such a pejorative label. I asked the Bishop to issue a directive discontinuing this term. Noting that he was a bit hesitant, I said, "Bishop, you'll have a *mitzvah*."

He laughed. "Touché," he said and issued the directive.

While I was working with the nuns, one of them told me a story about how she had chosen her vocation. When she was in grade school, some children received "indigent" books. The nun, Sister Edwina, told me that these books always had a red sticker on the back cover indicating they had to be returned at the end of the school year.

Kids can be cruel. Some would single out the children with the stickered books. "He gets the books from the county," the other kids would say, pointing out that the child was on the public dole. "I used to feel sorry for those kids who, through no fault of their own, were victims of these insults."

The Sister told me that she hated one teacher, a nun named Sister Rosamunde who was very stern. "She used to say we must pray for forgiveness even if we hadn't done anything, just in case we had sinful thoughts. How can a ten year old have sinful thoughts?"

But the next school year, her feelings changed. And this is why. In the beginning of the term Sister Rosamunde made all the children bring their books to her desk, "To be checked," she said. Rosamunde then put a red sticker on every single book. It became clear that Rosamunde's reference to sin was aimed at those kids who had taunted the poor students.

"That was when I first got the idea of being a teacher, which I am, as well as a nun."

The counseling program for the nuns continued for several years, until the readjustment to the new rules was in place. I came to admire these women, who had dedicated their lives to serving others.

Perhaps the greatest reward was the friendship I established with Cardinal Wright, a man of great knowledge, wisdom, and an enormous sense of humor. Incidentally, before I would take leave of him, the Cardinal would bow his head and say, "Bless me, Rabbi."

I am pleased that I was once able to bring cheer to the Cardinal, who suffered from a muscle-wasting disease, which threatened to cripple him. On one of our visits he was very dejected. "None of the doctors are frank with me," he said. "They are trying to spare my feelings. Can you please review my medical records and tell me the truth? I must know how progressive this disease is. If I will be unable to ambulate, I should not undertake responsibilities that I will be unable to execute."

"Stop worrying," I said. "When you are made Pope, they will carry you on a chair anyway." His enormous belly laugh told me that I had broken through his depression.

Good deeds can overcome denominational barriers. The Chassidic Rabbi, the Cardinal, the nuns. Ecumenics at its best.

Sometimes We Are the Divine
in Divine Intervention

The previous story reminds me of one other time I was the intermediary between God and one of us.

A thirty-four-year-old priest was admitted to St. Francis's for treatment for alcohol addiction. Unfortunately he had already begun to go into D.T.s, the acute alcohol withdrawal syndrome which can be fatal. He was put into intensive care and for days his heart rate did not go below two hundred beats per minute. He was so ill that he was anointed and given last rites. Somehow he managed to survive.

The day after he was transferred out of the ICU to a regular room he kept on requesting bottles of Cepacol mouthwash. At first he denied, but later admitted, drinking the mouthwash for its alcohol content. I told Father that if he was so addicted that he had to drink after nearly dying from alcohol, he would have to go on Antabuse daily, a medication which makes it impossible to drink without getting deathly sick.

"Can I take a sip of wine at Mass?" Father asked.

"No way," I said.

"Then I can't take Antabuse."

"Yes you can," I said. "Just use grape juice and you'll be able to say Mass."

"We can't use grape juice," Father said. "It must be wine."

I called my friend, Cardinal Wright, at the Vatican. "Cardinal," I said, "You must help me. This young priest is going to die. Please get him a dispensation to use grape juice for Mass."

"I will personally take this request to the Holy Father [Pope Paul VI]," Cardinal Wright replied.

"Tell the Pope I said he will have a *mitzvah*," I said.

Two days later Cardinal Wright called me. The Pope had instructed all alcoholic priests to use grape juice in the Mass.

The Pope had a *mitzvah*.

The Cardinal had a *mitzvah*.

I had a *mitzvah*.

And to this day, those priests in danger of relapse to alcohol addiction because of the Mass are saved.

A Golden Rule
That Proves the Exception

In the nineteenth century it was not uncommon for students and their teacher to travel in a group together if they were leaving school for the holidays. On one such trip, a young master and his teenage students stopped for the night at a small inn. For supper, they were served soup along with their dinner. The meal had been cooked and was served by a local girl who was new at her job.

When the first course of soup had been cleared the teacher immediately requested another bowl of soup. His students raised their eyebrows at this because the broth had tasted like dishwater and the vegetables were overcooked beyond recognition. "More soup, if you please," said the teacher after bowl number three.

Now the student to the teacher's right, Abraham, leaned over to the boy on his right, Benjamin, and said, "The master must be out of his mind. When does he ever have such an appetite?"

The long and short of this tale is that the master ate four bowls of terrible soup and of course had no room for meat or a sweet afterward. But by all appearances when he left the table he was just as content as if he'd eaten his own mother's home-cooked meal.

"Why did you ask for so much soup?" Abraham wanted to know. "It tasted terrible, surely you noticed." Abraham was at an age when young men can be callous and so he did not even bother to check to see if the young woman was nearby when he spoke. Luckily, the innkeeper's family and the staff of one were out of earshot.

"Abraham, I asked for the soup because it was terrible."

"What do you mean, Master?" Benjamin spoke for the group of five boys, all still mulling over this strange behavior.

"I finished all the soup purposely. If any other guests would have eaten it, they might have complained and the maid would have lost her job. This way, no one but us knows about the maid's cooking and perhaps she'll improve if she has more time to learn. I lost nothing by eating the soup except maybe my appetite for soup for a while. She would have lost so much more if she'd lost her job."

Be Cautious in Judging Others

In the village of Radomsk, there was a butcher who was considered to be a tightwad, rarely responding to any of the charitable activities in the community. In the town there was a soup kitchen where the hungry would go for meals. After the butcher died the kitchen was unable to provide meals and it was then discovered that the "tightwad" butcher had secretly been donating the food but did not want anyone to know it so that he would not run the risk of becoming egotistic about it. Apparently the butcher believed that it was not enough to be charitable, he also had to be careful not to toot his own horn over it. "Bounty always receives part of its value from the manner in which it is bestowed," said Samuel Johnson.

Chapter Seven

DOING FOR OTHERS FREES US FROM DESTRUCTIVE HABITS, FROM ANGER AND FEAR

Habit, n.: A shackle for the free.

AMBROSE BIERCE
The Devil's Dictionary

In a profound way, giving to and caring for others frees us from our most basic fears. The psychological truth is simple. Whenever we become too self-absorbed, and worry more about ourselves than about the people we love—mate, child, friend, parent—then we become vulnerable to our worst fears because we are constantly comparing ourselves to other people instead of feeling good about being ourselves.

Reaching out to others rids us of the fear, anxiety, and the preoccupation of worrying whether or not our needs will be met. When we give freely we cease to agitate over what we may get back in return.

Even so, some people are driven primarily by the pursuit of self-gratification. As the director of Gateway one of the most difficult issues I have had to address is this tyranny of desire. What I have witnessed is that the more a person falls prey to the demands of self, the more his uniquely human qualities disappear.

On the other hand, doing for others is a powerful tool for building the spirit. Acts of selfless kindness turn the soul outward, in the process breaking the worst of bad habits, freeing us from the seemingly unconquerable self-destructive needs and cravings of addiction.

According to the mythology of my family, a student once approached my forebear, the Rabbi of Rhizin, a learned and holy man, and asked him, "What principle can one follow in order to make correct decisions in one's everyday actions?"

After a moment's reflection, the Rabbi responded, "The answer is quite simple. The duty of a person is to overcome temptations. The tempter is always at work, and he seeks to seduce us through the cravings of our physical being. The principle to follow in order to resist is to act just as a tightrope walker maintains his balance, by tilting himself to the side opposite that to which he feels pulled. So can a person always make a right decision by acting opposite to that for which he feels himself craving."

And this is where the simple mechanics of doing unto others can play such a powerful role in helping a person to overcome even the worst habits. I have heard it said this way: the reason one should not sin is not because it is forbidden. Rather it is because one should be so busy doing for others that one simply doesn't have the time.

Do one good deed, and you begin to fill the empty space in the heart with goodness. The transition is easy—even the smallest good deed is enough to move one in the right direction. Anyone who is afraid of giving up his dependencies, whatever they are, only needs to take one little step toward another person, offer one selfless act of kindness, and the rest will follow. I know, from my more than twenty years' experience of helping people to overcome addiction, that this really works.

The body and spirit are in a tug of war with the body pulling toward instant fixes and the spirit fighting for devotion to matters outside the self. Twelve-step programs have been put together with kindness and charity to others included as tools for recovery. Any destructive habit is the self-will run riot. The breaking of these or any bad habits requires extending ourselves to help others in order to break the cycle of desire, gratification, more desire ...

A recovering cocaine addict I'll call John told me that after eight months of abstinence he was seized by an overwhelming craving to get high and started off to his supplier. Traveling along the highway in a light rain he saw a young couple with their two children standing outside their disabled car. He pulled over and after talking with them a bit, loaded the family into his car and drove them to his home. There he gave them all something to eat and called AAA to request a tow truck.

"After that," John said, "It was just out of the question for me to use cocaine that night. I can't say why exactly, but I just knew I couldn't."

Of course he couldn't. Cocaine is garbage and we only dump garbage into a garbage can. He had done a good deed, feeding his self-esteem. His body was no longer in his mind, a garbage can where he could dump anything that would be repulsive to his spirit.

Just Saying No to a Bad Habit May Not Be Enough. A Mitzvah May Help.

One of the stories I heard as a child was about a beggar who acquired a magic purse that contained a dollar. Whenever he removed a dollar, another dollar took its place. Three days later he was found dead, lying in a pile of dollars. Addiction to money may be as relentless as addiction to alcohol or drugs.

* * * * *

I used to lead a study group at a local synagogue and it was a terrific opportunity for me to share Chassidic teachings with this more traditional group. One time I relayed the teaching that there are moments of grace when a person receives Divine inspiration—the person may suddenly feel a strong desire to become more spiritual. Such moments of "spontaneous" inspiration are believed to be gifts from God.

The Chassidic masters taught that these rare moments are evanescent and that their inspiration soon fades so the opportunity to act on them must be seized.

The masters taught me and I taught the group that a person can seize these divine moments by performing a good deed. These deeds, it is said, are like vessels that retain these Divine inspirations.

After the study group that morning the congregants left and I remained behind. After a while, one of the group came back in and deposited several coins in the charity box. Then he turned to me and said, "I am a compulsive gambler. I've promised myself a hundred times that I would stop gambling, but I have never been able to keep my resolution. As I started to drive home today I thought that I must stop gambling and then I remembered what you said about Divine inspiration. I was determined not to let this time fade away. So I turned around and came back to give money to charity hoping that this deed might help me keep my resolution."

I engaged the man in conversation about his gambling problem and arranged for him to meet that very day with a recovered compulsive gambler who then introduced him to Gamblers Anonymous and he has remained abstinent to this day.

One day I ran into him and he took out a small purse from his pocket. "This is my own charity box. I am still prone to the impulse to gamble and I am not always able to reach someone for help. So I put a few coins in this little purse for charity and ask for God's help to keep me from relapsing. It's working," he said.

It is very little and yet enough for this man to feel better about himself from the very first day that he tried to break his habit. All he needed to do was put a few coins in a charity box.

Reach for the Light

A while back an adolescent from our treatment center ran away. He returned later on that night saying he had hitched a ride into town and was dropped off at the bus station. He didn't know where he was going, just that he had to run.

A woman asked him if he would help her carry her bags to the bus. He did this and then in a heartbeat made the decision to return to the treatment center. He told us he had not done any drugs but to my discredit, I did not believe him. Sure enough, he tested negative and I realized that I should spend more time practicing what I preach. The young man had done a good deed and this had caused him to reach for the light.

The Torn Prayer Shawl

For many years a rabbi had longed for a prayer shawl made of wool that came from the Holy Land. After much effort, he procured such a piece of wool, and gave it to one of his students to fashion it into a shawl.

Unfortunately, when he cut out the opening in the top of the shawl, the student had folded the cloth one time too many, so that instead of one hole there were two. The student realized that he had totally ruined the garment that his master had craved for so long. With great trepidation he showed his teacher the ruined wool, fully expecting a severe scolding for his negligence.

After looking at the cloth very sadly, and wiping away a tear from his eye, the teacher smiled at the young man. "It's quite all right," he said. "Do not fret."

"All right?" exclaimed his student. "But I have ruined your *talis*." "No, my child," the Rabbi said. "You see, it was *meant* to have two holes. The first is an opening for the head, and the second is to test whether I will lose my temper."

Restraining Can Be Gaining

To follow the Golden Rule, we should think about how awful it is to be at the receiving end of someone's outbursts; how it hurts to be called names, to be screamed at or abused. And we should not do this to others. Since we all goof occasionally, we have to remember when someone else makes a mistake at our expense that we do not wish to be humiliated and everyone else has the right not to be humiliated as well. When once as a child, I cursed at someone my father said that was unacceptable. The only malediction I was ever allowed to use, when really provoked, was: "May he have fresh, soft bread and cold, hard butter."

I once counseled an executive who was suffering from high blood pressure, a condition exacerbated by his terrible temper. I taught him the trick of defusing his anger with humor since rage and humor can not coexist. I learned this from a story told about Hillel, who was tested by a man who placed a bet that he could bring Hillel into rage. The man chose a time when Hillel needed to be undisturbed and pelted him with foolish questions. Hillel quietly responded to each question, saying, "Yes, my child, you ask well," and giving a reasonable answer to an absurd question. Many of these questions were absurd enough to require that Hillel strain to answer. For example, the man asked, "Why does the statue of the emperor need to be cleaned?" And Hillel then had to respond that the statue was cleaned by law for the same reason humans bathe, which is to show respect for the emperor and for oneself. A most obvious answer. Never did the sage lose his temper.

In his frustration over losing the bet the man said, "If you are a great man I hope there will not be many great men. You caused me to lose my bet!"

"The answer is not to wager," Hillel smiled. And then he took himself off to the baths, saying that he was respecting the law that caused both the emperor's statue and man to be clean.

* * * * *

The Rabbi of Gur was escorted to the train station by a group of his followers. Pointing to the train he said, "Do you know why that engine can pull so many heavy cars? Because it can control the enormous steam that builds up within it."

* * * * *

The philosopher Socrates' wife did not appreciate his wisdom and thought him to be a bit of a sloucher. Once she shouted at him, "Why aren't you going out to work? And if you must stay home, why aren't you helping with the house-work?" When the philosopher remained deep in thought and did not respond she threw a pitcher full of water at him. Socrates smiled and said, "I knew that after the thunder there would be rain." But he did not lose his temper.

Mitzvah *Beats Fear*

A psychiatrist, Viktor Frankl, describes his concentration camp experiences and tells of men who walked through the huts comforting others, giving away their last piece of bread. No doubt these men were very hungry themselves and giving up their meager ration was a major sacrifice. But the fear of being put to death was as lethal as the toxic fumes of the gas chambers. These men found that comforting others was a way to neutralize the paralyzing fear rampant in the camps.

The Light at the End of the Tunnel Is Courage

During World War II a family close to my own received the shocking news that their son was missing in action. The family was devastated and grieving. My father tried to keep their hopes up, reiterating frequently that MIA did not mean killed and that their son might be a prisoner of war or even lost only on paper in a bureaucratic snafu.

Every week my father visited the family each time trying to instill hope. He would enter their home smiling and exude confidence. He would say with great certainty that they would see their son alive and well. I know this because I accompanied my father on a few of these visits. After V-E Day the family was blessed with the news that their son had been a POW and was now well and on his way home.

When the soldier returned to his army base he found a stack of letters that had accumulated in his absence. These were from my father, who had written to him once a week for the two years that the boy was in captivity.

I know when my father wrote these letters. He did so each week just before he made his visit to the family. Writing the letters reinforced his own belief and strengthened his hope that the young man was indeed alive. Since he punched up his attitude, he could give hope to the family.

Of course my father feared the worst, but fear is destructive and so he combated it with the hope inherent in the writing of these letters. He continued to combat fear by communicating his confidence to the family. It was by the virtue of these acts that the family survived the ordeal.

The Only Fear
Is Losing Something

Rabbi Joseph Schneerson ran a seminary in Russia. When the Communists came to power they ordered all religious seminaries to close. Rabbi Schneerson defied the order and continued teaching religion. This continuance in and of itself was a superlative deed.

One day a government officer confronted him and ordered him to close his school, and he refused. The officer pulled out a gun and said, "You will close the school or you will be killed." Rabbi Schneerson showed no emotion and quietly responded, "The school will remain open."

The officer could not help being impressed by the Rabbi's calm demeanor and total lack of fear. "Don't you take me seriously?" he asked. "Aren't you afraid of dying?"

The Rabbi responded calmly, "Someone who has only one world and a multiplicity of gods is afraid of dying. Someone who has two worlds and only one God has no fear."

What the Rabbi was saying is that those who worship possessions or drugs, those who live to serve their own outlandish desires and so are too self-absorbed to see others, these people have much to worry about losing and therefore much to fear about death. But the person who serves God rather than living to indulge himself and who has only this world and heaven, and not all those other materialistic spheres in which to roam, that person has nothing to lose or to fear.

Rabbi Schneerson's yeshiva remained open, and in 1940 he transplanted it to the United States, where it took root and sent out shoots to all corners of the globe.

The guns of Russian communism have been silenced, whereas Rabbi Schneerson's teachings reverberate in the many educational centers he established. History has proven that he was right: it was the Communist officer and not the Rabbi that was in danger of losing his *raison d'être*.

Chapter Eight

GOOD DEEDS PROMOTE SPIRITUALITY

Anyone who has some good will find good everywhere.

AMOS OZ
Don't Call It Night

Once I was amazed to watch a school of salmon in a fishery on the Pacific coast. The fish would swim against the tide on their way upstream. When they encountered an obstacle, such as a cascade, they would leap to reach a higher level and continue on to an even more uphill course.

All programs for spiritual advancement advocate a gradual progression. Jacob dreamt of a ladder rooted in the earth and reaching into the heavens, a ladder with rungs to be ascended one at a time; recovery programs have twelve steps. And in our treatment center we have a poster which reads, "The elevator to recovery is out of order. Please use the twelve steps." Most spiritual people were not born that way, but achieved their spirituality through slow and steady attention to their soul's work. There is no high-speed journey to spirituality. It starts with setting a goal and using stepping-stones to get there. My advice is that those stones be good deeds.

If you are in search of spirituality, you have it. If you believe you already have it, you have lost it.

Home Run Lost Because There Was No Prayer—A True Story

I grew up in Milwaukee, which in those days was a minor-league town. But never mind, I still loved baseball. It cost a quarter to get in to Borchert Field.

My hero was Ted Gullic, number 22. He batted cleanup and was known as "old reliable." After the game we would rush down to catch the players before they went into the clubhouse and try to get an autograph. One time I actually caught Ted Gullic and asked for his autograph. "Will you hit a home run for me tomorrow?" I asked.

Ted looked me over, noticing my *yarmulke* (skullcap) and said, "You pray for me and I'll hit for you."

The next day I listened to the game and waited for the announcer to say, "There he goes!" hailing Ted Gullic's homer, but it didn't happen. Ted got a double and a single that day, that's all. In the postgame broadcast from the clubhouse, called *Tenth Inning*, Ted said, "I tried my hardest. I guess the kid that prayed for me didn't pray hard enough."

I have never forgotten Ted Gullic's reprimand. Today I pray for things much more important than a home run, such as for sick people to get well, and since I believe in the power of prayer, I try to pray ever harder. This incident was a defining moment in my spirituality; it taught me that people do count on our prayers and that it matters to pray with all your heart for the person who needs you.

Good Deed Equals Good Seed

Gaining a sense of spiritual well-being is much like enhancing the appearance of a living room by purchasing a new sofa. Once the sofa is in, the room looks prettier but the carpet looks a bit shabbier than it did before. Now we replace the carpet and the drapes do not go with the new carpet and they must be replaced, then of course the drapes don't go with the wallpaper and so on. By the time we have added new lamps, chairs, a coffee table and knickknacks there is a totally new room which came into being because of a single new piece of furniture.

Imagine each of these improvements is a good deed. Each *mitzvah* provides illumination and the more light there is, the more one can discover spots that need cleaning. Some people may think that only a lifetime of virtue will earn them entry to Paradise. We can acquire Paradise in just one moment. The Talmud cites an example of a person who was an immoral degenerate his entire life and at the very end repented with his whole heart. He was immediately assured a place in Paradise.

The performance of one deed rearranges our spirit. Soon we're looking for good deeds to do, not just waiting passively for the need to fall in our laps. After that we are moving into the performance of deeds that require more of us and leave us feeling better all the time. The more we nurture our spirit the closer we get to recognizing our path in this world, our mission. If we make a point to redecorate our spirits continually we will flourish and grow.

This reminds me of a story of the patriarch Abraham sitting outside the door of his tent, looking for wayfarers to whom he could be of help or at the least be hospitable. His spirituality had so evolved that ingrained in his character was the impulse to seek out those in need, rather than only responding.

God, Too, Does Mitzvahs

A religious man was walking with his disciples when they came upon a small child crying. "Why are you crying?" the master asked. "We are playing hide and seek," the child answered. "I hid myself but none of my friends are looking for me."

The master turned to his students and said, "Can you imagine the distress of God who has concealed Himself in the world, in the works of nature, and no one tries to find Him? Can you imagine how that grieves Him?"

God wants us to find him. Sometimes he gives us hints where He is in the hope that we will look for him. These hints are His way of encouraging us to come closer. These are God's *mitzvahs*.

Pay attention to the little things that "happen" to you. How many times did the right thing just "happen" which saved you time, money, or prevented you from illness or injury? These are God's hints. Yes, God does *mitzvahs*, He follows the Golden Rule. When we go to look for Him, we grow closer, we halt God's grieving.

God Needs Love Too

The following story demonstrates how simple it can be to acknowledge God's good deeds.

There was a shepherd who taught the Baal Shem Tov, the mystic master, about spiritual growth. The Master, who was on his own quest, was told of a shepherd who had achieved a higher level of spirituality than even he, the Baal Shem Tov. Always willing to learn and advance, the Master took some of his disciples and went to find the shepherd. They discovered the young man in the pasture tending his flock and they concealed themselves to observe him without disturbing him.

Soon enough the shepherd took out his flute and said, "Great God, you created this whole world with these beautiful trees, green meadows, the flowing brook, and the white clouds in the azure sky. How can I show You my appreciation?" And with that, he took out his flute and played beautiful melodies.

"That is not enough for a great God like You. I will do somersaults." And this he did, deftly turning.

Then the shepherd said, "I have played the flute and done somersaults, yet I still feel I want to give God something. All I have is this small coin," whereupon he took the coin and hurled it toward the sky.

The Baal Shem Tov said to his disciples, "You will not see that coin fall to the ground. It is a fine gift this young man gives to God and it will give the shepherd a place in Heaven."

Prayer Is Powerful

There can only be one goal in life which dominates while every other goal takes second place. An excellent beginning technique for defining a goal and planning how to get there is prayer. This is the first step to stretching spirituality as well. When we pray for something not only are we going to receive some sort of "feedback" from God, but we also clarify the goal as we verbalize it in our prayer. But I don't want to pray, you might say. One recovering alcoholic I know, an avowed atheist, had difficulty following AA's program. However, after some time he was able to pray. When asked if he "believed" now in prayer he said, "I did not believe in God when I started praying and I don't believe in Him now. But when I pray that reminds me that I am not God."

Once a goal or mission is found, praying for help in reaching it reminds us we have not yet arrived and that achieving a goal is not a spontaneous happening. Prayer also motivates. It serves, too, as a declaration of what one is looking for.

Sometimes we harbor toxic feelings that we want to be rid of, yet try as we might, it seems impossible to overcome these gut-level emotions. There is a solution: say a prayer, or do something nice for him or her. Whenever we do something for another we acquire interest in that person. We have invested in him. And it is only natural that we protect our interest. In this way we automatically change these feelings into benign ones, and along the way grow spiritually.

Transformation of Feelings
Via Mitzvahs

A few days before I had finished putting this book together I was trapped on a plane. First we were ready to take off, then the captain announced a brief delay while maintenance fixed something trivial. The delay extended to an hour. Suddenly the flight was canceled and we were shepherded off the plane.

I was angry. I had speaking engagements in two different cities and was already exhausted from the two cities' worth of engagements that had come the week before.

I didn't like the way I was feeling and thought about what I was writing here, about how spirituality grows in us. At that moment a patient of mine came to mind, a woman who was being treated for a brain tumor and had undergone a marked personality change. When I saw her, she had cussed me out. I knew this wasn't her fault but still it is never pleasant to be insulted.

I decided at that moment to give her a call. I got her number from information and when I got her on the phone she was very nice and thankful for the call. I had done a good deed, and found when I hung up that my anger over the flight was completely dissipated. It worked! I had used a good deed to turn my negativity around.

We're All God's Children

Rabbi Elimelech was a saintly person who felt that he must do penance for his "sins." He therefore left the comfort of his home for a self-imposed exile, wandering from village to village, often sleeping in the fields and subsisting on whatever food he might find.

After an extended period he returned home and upon meeting the first person of the village inquired after the welfare of his family.

"Your boy, Eliezer, is sick," the man said. Rabbi Elimelech rushed home and breathlessly asked his wife, "What is wrong with Eliezer?"

"Nothing is wrong with him," his wife said. "He is in school."

"But I was told he was sick."

"Oh, yes," his wife said, "One of the neighbors' children, also named Eliezer, is sick."

At first the rabbi felt relief, but then he admonished himself, "With all your spirituality you still are glad when it is a child other than your own that is ill. What difference does it make if it is your Eliezer or someone else's?" He bade his wife farewell and returned to exile in an effort to improve on his defective spirituality. In this way, Rabbi Eliezer took the words "Love thy neighbor as thyself" literally. Though we should not expect ourselves to go to such lengths it's a good idea to learn from his example. Loving his son, the Rabbi knew, should extend in some way to his community.

As Napoleon Hill says, "There is no seed of bad which does not contain an equivalent or greater amount of good."

Grandma Used to Call Them Growing Pains

I once read a fascinating account of how a lobster grows. It carries its shell until it outgrows it, at which point the crustacean crawls to a safe place, sheds the outgrown shell and must live exposed until the new shell grows in. The lobster, which can live for many years, must go through this process over and over, always growing out of its shell and then having to expose its soft, vulnerable places until a new casing grows in again.

It's lucky that lobsters don't have a doctor to prescribe Valium to eliminate their discomfort due to this oppressive shell. There would never be big lobsters! I remember how grandmother would always dismiss our bellyaching, saying, "It's just growing pains."

Of course when we feel stressed we may be sullen, irritable or impatient. This makes me think of how vulnerable we all must be in those times when we are growing spiritually, intellectually and emotionally. It is at these times that it is probably most important to be aware of our actions toward others. If we are good to others when we are vulnerable, they will treat us with sensitivity in turn. This applies person to person, community to community, country to country, it applies across the board and as the community of mankind becomes ever more vulnerable it is increasingly imperative to treat each other as we would be treated ourselves.

The Ultimate Good Deed Story

Why do countless people come to the Western Wall in Jerusalem to pray? What is it that makes this particular place so receptive to our prayers? There was a temple here once, destroyed many centuries ago. Now only the Western Wall of the temple remains. There is a story about this place and within this story is the answer to why so many people pray here. It is perhaps the ultimate good deed story.

Long ago there were two brothers who inherited a field from their father and divided it equally. One brother was childless while the other had a large family. When the grain from the field was harvested, the brother with the large family thought, "My brother is sad because he has no children. Perhaps I can raise his spirits by giving him a little extra grain. After all, people are happier when they have a bit more."

So during the night when all were asleep, he took several sheaves of grain and put them in his brother's storing place.

The childless brother, meanwhile, was thinking to himself, "For my wife and myself I have enough grain. My brother has a large family and needs more than we do." So during the night, when all were asleep, he took several sheaves of grain and put them in his brother's storing place.

This exchange continued until one night the brothers met and their secrets were exposed. They embraced tearfully and swore that their love for each other would never perish.

God looked down at this scene and said, "Here, at this place where the brothers met and embraced there will be a Sanctuary where prayers will be heard, and not just said." And this became the site for the Temple, where only the Western Wall now remains.

The Western Wall is known also as the Wailing Wall. True, many weep there for those they have lost. But we do not cry for the past alone, we cry also for the present, for brothers who should be embracing and trying to help one another but who are killing each other in senseless and ruthless selfishness.

On occasion you may find people dancing joyously at the Wailing Wall. If it is a place to weep, how can it be a place to rejoice? Remember Chaim-Cheskel, the itinerant rabbi. There is always a part within us that has thanks and hope.

Just as the brothers of the legend were devoted to each other and found happiness in doing for each other so there is a part of us that always hopes that humankind will yet discover its kinship and embrace rather than destroy one another.

This is why people pray at a site that once was a field and then a sanctuary that was destroyed in war. Because two brothers gave unto each other selflessly, God called for a Sanctuary that, though destroyed, still calls to us with its holiness because goodness is stronger, the brothers' deeds are stronger than war. Wars may last for decades whereas the legacy of goodness can endure forever.

A heathen approached the sage Rabbi Hillel some two thousand years ago and said that he wanted to convert to Judaism. But the heathen said he was very busy and would consider it only if the Rabbi could teach him everything he needed to know about the religion while the proselyte stood on one foot.

Rabbi Hillel directed the man to stand on one foot.

Said Hillel: "What is hateful to you, do not do to your neighbor. That is the whole of the Torah, the rest is commentary."

This is not a long book—in fact it is quite short—short enough to read even while standing on one foot.

Hillel essentially says, "*Mitzvah* begets *mitzvah*." Once you do one, sooner than you would think, there will be another and another. . . . You'll find yourself feeling good, doing ever more good.

And that is all you ever need to know.